small bites

small bites

tapas, sushi, mezze, antipasti, and other finger foods

Jennifer Joyce

LONDON, NEW YORK, MELBOURNE, MUNICH, DELHI

This book is dedicated to Deidre, my lovely sister

Project Editor Jennifer Lane
Project Art Editor Sara Robin
Designer Andrew Barron
Senior Editor Jennifer Jones
Managing Editors Stephanie Farrow, Penny Warren
Managing Art Editor Marianne Markham
Publishing Manager Gillian Roberts
Art Director Carole Ash
Publishing Director Mary-Clare Jerram
DTP Designer Sonia Charbonnier
Production Controller Stuart Masheter
Photographer Sian Irvine
US Editors Jennifer Williams, Nicole Turney, Christine Heilman
US Recipe Consultant Wesley Martin

First American Edition 2005

Published in the United States by
DK Publishing, Inc., 375 Hudson Street
New York, New York 10014

05 06 07 08 09 10 9 8 7 6 5 4 3 2 1

Copyright © 2005 Dorling Kindersley Limited
Text copyright © 2005 Jennifer Joyce

A Catalog record for this book is available from the Library of Congress.
ISBN 0-7566-1347-7

Reproduced by Colourscan (Singapore)
Printed and bound in China by South China Printing Co. Ltd (China)

Discover more at
www.dk.com

Contents

Introduction

There's a revolution going on. The formality of the dining room table is being exchanged for a more relaxed gathering around the coffee table as the new mode for entertaining. Growing numbers of home cooks are unashamedly offering guests simply a selection of canapés and appetizers as a main meal. They are dismissing the classic three-course scenario, with large cuts of meat or fish, in favor of diminutive yet beguiling bites.

Depending on where you happen to be, these little dishes may be called tapas, mezze, antipasti, or simply finger food. But no matter what their origin, they share a tantalizing similarity—an amalgamation of salty, sweet, sour, and spicy flavors. Once our palates are woken with such tastes, we can't help but crave more.

Delicious taste is not the only reason for this coffee-table movement; lifestyle also plays a part. An evening spent surrounded by a myriad of exotic dishes promotes a more sociable, relaxed atmosphere than when plodding through multiple, formal courses.

This especially suits those who want to entertain stylishly, but live in small spaces and without a dining table. The growing popularity of book clubs and casual gatherings of friends is starting to change the way we entertain and cook.

Small Bites is an inspirational book that takes glorious license in experimenting with bold tastes, such as chili peppers, spices, garlic, anchovies, and fresh herbs. People are now traveling farther afield and more frequently and want to recreate their newly discovered tastes at home and with ease. As a teacher of popular

Chunky chopped salad with red wine and caper vinaigrette (see p74)

Crab and Gruyère nachos with charred tomato salsa (see p142)

classes on modern ethnic cuisines such as Moorish, Middle Eastern, Pacific, and Southeast Asian cooking, I have a real understanding of how to create exotic appetizers that are the most delicious and novel parts of a meal. Don't fear any ingredients that are new to you—there are useful websites (*see p223*) to help you.

To answer the needs of home cooks at all levels, the recipes offer comprehensive advice for think-ahead preparation, along with suggestions for accompaniments that will balance both flavor and time involved. Inventive menu plans and cocktail ideas that suit a theme of a specific cuisine, such as Japanese or Mediterranean, are scattered throughout the book to help inspire you. On these pages I have created a timeline to help you plan out the preparation.

Since some dishes are more labor-intensive than others, there are six quick recipe features offering suggestions for simple dishes. Use these to add complementary recipes to your menu without placing an unrealistic demand on your time.

Peking seared duck rolls with plum sauce
(see p180)

Raspberry meringues with white chocolate swirls
(see p208)

This book is a gathering of my favorite recipes that are innovative, approachable, and, most importantly, have the "wow factor." I hope you enjoy making them as much as I enjoyed creating them. Whether you select dishes solely as appetizers or create an entire menu from them, you will not fail to impress and delight your friends.

Jennifer Joyce

Sizzling, golden, and mouthwateringly crisp—when fried food beckons, it's impossible to show restraint. Creamy dips or sticky chili pepper sauces add to the taste experience. This tempting, rich food is set apart from everyday fare and perfect for special occasions. Think of these tasty morsels as treats to be savored without remorse.

Fried

Fried artichokes, Roman style
with saffron aioli

These artichokes resemble exotic flowers after they're fried, and they are as good to eat as they are to look at. Use baby ones, seasonal in spring and fall, since they'll require far less time to prepare than their larger globe counterparts.

1 Fill a medium-sized bowl with water and add the lemon juice. Pull the tough outer leaves from the artichokes until you reach the pale, tender leaves inside. Trim the stems back to 2 in (5 cm). Using a vegetable peeler, peel the sides and ends of the stems. Using a melon baller, scoop out the fuzzy choke inside the artichokes and discard. Place the artichokes in the water to prevent discoloring.

2 Preheat the oven to 300°F (150°C). Heat a wok or small, heavy-bottomed saucepan. Add the oil and heat until a small cube of bread, dropped in, sizzles immediately. Remove three artichokes from the water, drain on paper towels, and flatten the tops by pressing them face-down on the countertop. Lower into the wok or pan, fry until golden, and drain on paper towels. Keep warm while you fry the remaining artichokes. Serve sprinkled with salt and accompanied by the saffron aioli.

Prepare ahead
The aioli can be made the night before and refrigerated. The artichokes can be peeled the night before, kept in the lemon water, and refrigerated. They can then be fried up to 30 minutes before and kept warm in a preheated oven at 300°F (150°C).

INGREDIENTS

Juice of 2 lemons

20 baby artichokes

1⅔ cups peanut or vegetable oil

1 tsp salt

1 recipe saffron aioli (*see p217*), to serve

Preparation time 40 minutes

Makes 20 pieces

BUY AND ARRANGE

Baby shrimp with arugula (*see p149*) • roasted garlic with warm bread (*see p71*) • chocolate hazelnut spread on toasted brioche (*see p214*)

PARTNER WITH

Wild mushroom crostini (*see p153*) • seared beef carpacico (*see p128*) • rosemary lamb chops (*see p118*) • strawberries and figs (*see p207*)

Coconut shrimp
with mango mint dipping sauce

This tangy combination provides a fresh blend of flavors and works well for a menu based on Middle Eastern, Indian, or Pacific themes. The shrimp can also be paired successfully with other dips (see p216–19).

1 Preheat the oven to 300°F (150°C). Wash and dry the shrimp on paper towels. Put the corn starch, beaten egg whites, and coconut in three separate bowls. Season the shrimp with salt and pepper, then dip into the corn starch. Shake off the excess, then dip into the egg white, and finally into the coconut.

2 Heat the oil in a large wok or heavy, medium-sized saucepan over medium-high heat. To tell if the oil is hot enough to deep fry the shrimp, drop a small piece of bread into the oil—if it sizzles it's ready.

3 Deep-fry the shrimp in the oil until golden, about 6 at a time. Drain on paper towels and keep warm in the oven until ready to serve. Accompany with the mango mint dipping sauce and garnish with lime zest, if desired.

Prepare ahead
The shrimp can be coated 1 hour before frying and kept in the refrigerator. After frying, they can be kept warm in a preheated oven at 300°F (150°C) up to 30 minutes before serving.

INGREDIENTS

1 lb (450 g) medium-sized or large shrimp, peeled and deveined

1 cup corn starch

4 egg whites, lightly beaten

1¼ cups unsweetened dried coconut

Salt and pepper

2½ cups peanut or vegetable oil

1 recipe mango mint dipping sauce (see p216)

Zest of 1 lime, for garnish (optional)

Preparation time 35 minutes
Makes 20 large or 30 medium shrimp, depending on size

BUY AND ARRANGE

Crab and cream cheese dip (see p71) • mango fool (see p215) • freshly sliced watermelon (see p215)

PARTNER WITH

Seared cinnamon duck (see p124) • red curry pumpkin soup (see p46) • raspberry meringues (see p208)

Colors

- Vivid turquoise
- Lime green
- Berry red
- Lemon yellow
- Hot pink

Tableware

- Bubble-glass plates
- Strings of lights
- Hand-painted plates
- Multicolored tablecloths
- Rainbow-striped napkins

Latin fiesta

Celebratory in spirit but relaxed in presentation, Latin food invites warm and generous entertaining. Spicy, sour, and sometimes sweet, the flavors of this cuisine are complex yet unpretentious. Creamy avocados, smoky chili peppers, and sour limes are a few of its iconic ingredients.

No other cuisine in the world uses as many dried and fresh chili peppers, each with its own particular characteristics. Some have a wine-fruity taste, others are smoky, tobacco-like, or chocolatey. If I had to choose a favorite pepper, it would be the chipotle—a jalapeño that is smoked during drying and then reconstituted in a garlicky tomato sauce. This pepper adds magic smokiness to salsas, marinades, or dips. Find a good online supplier (*see Useful Addresses p223*) and buy a few cans of them at a time to keep your home stocked.

Think colorful and festive when setting the table for a Latin evening. Bubble-glass crockery is a Mexican classic, in blues and greens. Use any hand-painted plates you may have, especially those with vivid, colorful designs. A good assortment of brightly-colored linens will help set the tone. Homemade salty margaritas are a must for this feast.

Flavors

- Chili peppers—fresh and dried
- Cool sour cream
- Sharp limes
- Creamy avocados
- Garlicky sauces and salsas

Nibbles

- Warm spicy almonds (*see p30*)
- Salsa with tortilla chips (*see p70*)
- Pan-fried padron peppers (*see p30*)
- Escabeche of carrots (*see p216*)
- Marinated black olives (*see p30*)

Menu

Chili pepper gazpacho
with sourdough croutons

Broiled butterfly shrimp
with butter, lime, and jalapeño

Crispy chorizo quesadillas
with guacamole

Soft-shell steak tacos
with smoky tomatillo salsa

Serrano-rolled asparagus
with saffron aioli

Chocolate crinkle cookies
with walnuts

BUY AND ARRANGE

Watermelon and feta salad
(see p93)

Pan-fried padron peppers
(see p30)

Warm spicy almonds
(see p30)

Chili pepper gazpacho
(see p36)

Broiled butterfly shrimp
(see p141)

Crispy chorizo quesadillas
(see p186)

Soft-shell steak tacos
(see p178)

Serrano-rolled asparagus
(see p152)

Chocolate crinkle cookies
(see p204)

Two days before
- Make carrot escabeche
- Make chocolate cookies

The night before
- Make gazpacho and croutons
  but keep separate
- Clean and butterfly shrimp
- Make saffron aioli
- Make tomatillo salsa
- Marinate steaks for tacos

In the morning
- Squeeze limes for margaritas
- Chop ingredients for broiled
  butterfly prawns
- Make guacamole
- Make Serrano-rolled asparagus

Classic margarita

Buy a tequila that is 100% agave, if you can. This ensures quality and will minimize the risk of a headache the next day.

INGREDIENTS

Coarse salt

1 lime, cut into wedges

8 fl oz (1 cup) 100% agave tequila

8 fl oz (1 cup) orange liqueur, such as Cointreau

8 fl oz (1 cup) fresh lime juice

5 tbsp sugar

1 large handful of ice

Makes 8 generous margaritas

Scatter salt onto a plate. Rub the rims of each glass with the lime wedges, then dip each into the salt to coat. Pour the remaining ingredients into a blender or cocktail shaker, and blend or shake well. Pour into glasses and add more ice to the glasses if desired.

One hour before
- Assemble quesadillas; leave uncooked
- Grill onions for tacos
- Blend or shake margaritas
- Pour gazpacho into cups; refrigerate
- Make watermelon salad; keep dressing separate

Half an hour before
- Cook quesadillas
- Grill steaks for tacos
- Cook padron peppers; plate
- Plate chocolate cookies
- Pan-fry almonds; plate
- Plate Serrano-rolled asparagus

At the last minute
- Blend margaritas again; pour
- Broil butterfly shrimp; plate
- Plate quesadillas
- Plate steak tacos
- Plate watermelon salad with dressing
- Serve gazpacho with croutons

Crispy vegetable pakoras
with tamarind and ginger dipping sauce

Pakoras are one of the few fried snacks that can be prepared well in advance and retain their crunchy coating. Graham flour can be found in the Indian section of most supermarkets (see useful addresses, p223).

1 Preheat the oven to 400°F (200°C). Combine the flours, spices, and salt with the water, and beat to a smooth batter. The mixture should be thick, so add additional flour if necessary.

2 Pour the oil into a heavy-bottom, medium-sized saucepan or large wok that will maintain the heat level. Heat until a small piece of bread, when dropped in, sizzles immediately.

3 Dip the vegetable pieces into the batter one at a time, then drop into the hot oil. Deep-fry up to 6 pieces at a time, but don't overcrowd the saucepan. Cook for 3–4 minutes, until golden. Remove from the oil with a slotted spoon, and drain on paper towels. Keep warm in the oven until ready to serve. Garnish with the mint and serve with the ginger and tamarind dipping sauce.

Prepare ahead

The pakoras can be fried up to 4 hours ahead, kept at room temperature, and then reheated for 5 minutes in an oven preheated to 400°F (200°C). The sauce can be made up to 3 days ahead and refrigerated.

INGREDIENTS

¼ cup graham flour, plus extra if necessary (see method)

⅓ cup self-rising flour

½ tsp garam masala

¼ tsp ground cumin

¼ tsp ground turmeric

¼ tsp chili powder

½ tsp salt

⅔ cup water

4 cups peanut or vegetable oil

25 very thin slices of any of these vegetables: onion, potato, eggplant, baby artichoke, green beans, or fennel

Tamarind and ginger dipping sauce (see p219), to serve

Mint sprigs, to garnish

Preparation time 15 minutes
Cooking time 15 minutes
Makes around 25 pieces

BUY AND ARRANGE	PARTNER WITH
Tomato and coconut sambal (see p93) • selection of chutneys and pickles (see p70) • Indian sugar-coated fennel seeds (see p215)	Halibut parcels (see p146) • tomato and ginger soup (see p50) • raspberry meringues (see p208)

Mozzarella en carrozza
with capers

A grilled cheese sandwich seems uninspired next to these tasty bites from Naples. Sourdough or Campagne bread need not be authentic but will ensure that every bite is chewy.

1 Cut the mozzarella into ½-in (1-cm) thick slices. Divide evenly between 5 slices of bread. Sprinkle with the capers and top with the remaining bread. Slice the crusts off the sandwiches.

2 In a bowl, beat together the eggs, milk, salt, and pepper. Heat the butter and olive oil in a nonstick sauté pan over medium-low heat. Dip the sandwiches, two at a time, into the egg mixture. Fry for about 2 minutes on each side, until golden, then drain on paper towels. Cut into quarters and serve.

Prepare ahead

The egg mixture can be prepared 3 hours ahead and refrigerated. The sandwiches can be fried and kept warm in a preheated oven at 325°F (160°C) for 30 minutes before serving.

INGREDIENTS

1 lb (450 g) fresh mozzarella, drained and at room temperature

10 thin slices sourdough or Campagne bread

1 tbsp small capers, rinsed

2 large eggs, beaten

¼ cup milk

1 tsp salt

½ tsp black pepper

1 tbsp butter

1 tbsp olive oil

Preparation time 15 minutes

Cooking time 20 minutes

Makes 20 sandwiches

BUY AND ARRANGE

Pan-fried chorizo (see p149) • marinated anchovies (see p30) • fig, prosciutto, and mozzarella salad (see p92)

PARTNER WITH

Bagna cauda dip (see p54) • farro salad (see p78) • artichoke puff pastry bites (see p196)

Chunky eggplant sticks
with parmesan

Uncomplicated yet utterly addictive, these plump eggplant sticks are presoaked in water to keep them crispy, yet still full and juicy, once fried.

1 Place the eggplant sticks in a large bowl of cold water and soak for 1 hour. Heat the olive oil over medium-high heat in a wok or medium-sized, heavy-bottomed saucepan. It will be hot enough when a small piece of eggplant, dropped in, sizzles immediately.

2 Spread the flour on a plate. Lift the eggplant sticks from the water, dip into the flour to coat, then shake off the excess. Fry 4–6 sticks at a time, until golden brown, and drain on paper towels. Sprinkle with the salt, pepper, and Parmesan. Serve with the lemon wedges.

Prepare ahead

The eggplant can be fried and kept in a preheated oven at 325°F (160°C) for 30 minutes before serving.

INGREDIENTS

2 large eggplants, trimmed and cut into ¾-in (2-cm) sticks

1½ cups vegetable oil

1 cup all-purpose flour

1 tsp each salt and pepper

6 tbsp finely grated Parmesan

Lemon wedges, to serve

Preparation time 5 minutes, plus 1 hour soaking
Cooking time 15 minutes
Makes 20–30 sticks

BUY AND ARRANGE

Radicchio, orange, and arugula salad (*see p92*) • marinated olives (*see p30*) • biscotti, mascarpone, and dessert wine (*see p215*)

PARTNER WITH

Baby clams (*see p136*) • bresaola and pear rolls (*see p188*) • chocolate Frangelico pudding (*see p200*)

Crispy scallops
with wasabi mayonnaise

These sweet scallops are light, versatile, and work well with most sauces, so use your imagination (*see pp216–19*). Instead of ordinary breadcrumbs, try the panko variety. They can be found in Asian and gourmet food shops.

1 Season the scallops with the salt and pepper. Put the flour, eggs, and breadcrumbs in three separate bowls. Dip the scallops in the flour. Shake off the excess, then dip in the egg, and finally in the breadcrumbs. Keep refrigerated until ready to fry.

2 Heat a wok or small, heavy-bottomed saucepan. Pour in the oil and heat until a breadcrumb, dropped in, sizzles immediately. Deep-fry the scallops, 3 or 4 at a time, until golden. Drain on paper towels. Slice the green onion into fine julienne and curl with the edge of a knife. Serve the cakes warm, garnished with green onion curls and lime wedges, and accompanied by the sauces.

Prepare ahead

The scallops can be coated and sauces prepared in the morning of serving day and stored in the refrigerator.

INGREDIENTS

20 medium-sized or large scallops, with corals removed

½ tsp salt

½ tsp pepper

1 cup all-purpose flour

2 eggs, beaten

1¼ cups toasted breadcrumbs or panko breadcrumbs

1⅔ cups peanut or vegetable oil

Green onion, to garnish

Lime wedges, to serve

1 recipe wasabi mayonnaise (*see p219*) and/or ponzu soy dipping sauce (*see p217*)

Preparation time 35 minutes
Makes 20 pieces

BUY AND ARRANGE

Roasted asparagus with soy (*see p172*) • watercress sald with spring onion (*see p93*) • selection of sushi (*see p31*)

PARTNER WITH

Sticky chicken wings (*see p126*) • roasted butternut squash (*see p162*) • coconut macaroons (*see p210*)

Thai corn fritters
with chili pepper and cilantro sauce

The quintessential late-summer vegetable, corn kernels cut fresh from the cob have an intense flavor. Self-rising flour is the secret to making these fritters fluffy and light.

1 Cut the kernels from the cobs and place in a medium-sized bowl. Stir in both types of flour, the chili powder, scallions, salt, and pepper. Gradually beat in the beer to form a batter. Mix well and leave to rest for at least 30 minutes.

2 Pour the oil into a thick, heavy-bottomed, medium-sized saucepan or large wok. Heat until a small piece of bread, dropped in, sizzles instantly. Drop in the batter, 1 tablespoon at a time, and fry the fritters in batches of about 6 for around 5 minutes, until golden and crispy. Drain on paper towels. Garnish with the cilantro and serve hot with the sauce.

Prepare ahead
The batter can be prepared 3 hours in advance and refrigerated. The chili pepper sauce can be made 2 days ahead and refrigerated. Alternatively, the fritters may be fried and frozen, then thawed in the refrigerator and baked for 5 minutes in an oven preheated to 400°F (200°C).

INGREDIENTS

5 fresh corn cobs

1 cup all-purpose flour

½ cup self-rising flour

1 tsp chili powder

4 scallions, finely sliced

½ tsp each salt and pepper

1 cup beer

2 cups vegetable or peanut oil

Cilantro, to garnish

1 recipe chili pepper and cilantro sauce (see p218) or bottled sweet chili pepper dipping sauce, to serve

Preparation time 10 minutes
Cooking time 30 minutes
Makes 24 fritters

BUY AND ARRANGE

Crab and cream cheese dip (see p71) • selection of sushi (see p31) • fresh unpeeled lychees (see p215)

PARTNER WITH

Seared duck and mango salad (see p90) • five spice hoisin ribs (see p132) • passion fruit trifle (see p206)

Ithaca zucchini cakes
with dill yogurt sauce

The breadcrumbs keep these vegetable cakes plump and crisp. The cakes are equally tempting hot or at room temperature, with the refreshing dill yogurt for dipping.

1 To remove excess moisture from the zucchini, grate, sprinkle with the salt, and leave in a colander for 30 minutes. Meanwhile, preheat the oven to 375°F (190°C). Reserve 8 tablespoons of breadcrumbs, spread the remaining breadcrumbs on a nonstick baking sheet, and bake for 10 minutes, stirring a couple of times, until golden and crisp. Set aside to cool.

2 Rinse the zucchini and squeeze with your hands to remove as much liquid as possible, or the cakes will be too wet. Spread on a clean dish towel and blot with another. Mix the zucchini with the onions, eggs, feta, reserved breadcrumbs, mint, and nutmeg, and season with salt and pepper. Using floured hands, form the mixture into 15–18 plump, round 2-in- (5-cm-) wide patties. Press the patties into the toasted breadcrumbs, making sure they are coated all over.

3 Heat a frying pan over medium-high heat. Add enough olive oil to submerge half of each patty, and heat until a small piece of bread, dropped in, sizzles immediately. Fry the patties for about 3 minutes on each side, until crisp and golden. Drain on paper towels. Serve with the yogurt sauce and lemon wedges.

Prepare ahead
The cakes can be fried 2 hours before serving and reheated for 5 minutes in an oven preheated to 400°F (200°C). The dill yogurt sauce can be prepared in the morning of serving day.

INGREDIENTS

1 lb (500 g) small zucchini, trimmed

1 tbsp salt

1¾ cups fine fresh breadcrumbs

6 green onions, finely chopped

2 eggs, lightly beaten

⅔ cup feta cheese, crumbled

½ cup fresh mint leaves, chopped

¼ tsp nutmeg

Salt and freshly ground pepper, to taste

A little flour for shaping

Olive oil, for frying

1 recipe dill yogurt sauce (*see p216*), to serve

Lemon wedges, to serve

Preparation time 30 minutes
Cooking time 12 minutes
Makes 15–18 small cakes

BUY AND ARRANGE

Tomato and feta skewers (*see p31*) • Middle Eastern pastries (*see p214*) • frisée with quail's eggs (*see p93*)

PARTNER WITH

Roasted shrimp and tomatoes (*see p145*) • beet pesto (*see p67*) • chunky chopped salad (*see p74*)

Quick nibbles
buy-and-arrange ideas for quick-to-prepare snacks

These quick nibbles are perfect to serve at the beginning of the evening while your guests are arriving. The recipes are devilishly addictive, especially the caramelized nuts and crostinis. Choose your nibbles according to the theme of the evening, how much time you have left to prepare food, and the drinks you are serving.

Marinated olives

There are two olive recipes; with both, leave to marinate for 30 minutes to an hour, then serve. Olive mix 1: mix together 2 handfuls of good-quality, large, pitted green olives, 2 finely chopped tender stalks of celery, 1 teaspoon fennel seeds, and 1 clove garlic, finely sliced. Olive mix 2: mix together 2 handfuls of good-quality, pitted black olives, 2 strips of orange zest, 1 clove garlic, crushed, and 1 teaspoon dried oregano.

Pan-fried padron peppers

Heat 1 tablespoon olive oil in a nonstick frying pan until hot and pan-fry 3–4 handfuls of small sweet green peppers, such as padrons, for about 4 minutes. Shake the pan regularly to prevent sticking. Serve on small plates, sprinkled with flaked sea salt.

Marinated anchovies

Buy about ¼ lb (125 g) fresh anchovies, and place in a serving dish. Drizzle with 1 teaspoon red wine vinegar and 1 tablespoon extra-virgin olive oil. Sprinkle with 1 tablespoon freshly chopped parsley, then season with salt and pepper.

Caramelized nuts

In a baking pan, mix 2 large handfuls of nuts, such as pecans, hazelnuts, or walnuts, with 4 tablespoons maple syrup, 2 tablespoons sugar, ½ teaspoon cayenne pepper, and 1 tablespoon extra-virgin olive oil. Bake for 10 minutes at 350°F (180°C), then allow to cool on a nonstick surface. To create an Asian flavor, add 1 teaspoon soy sauce.

Spanish or Italian deli plate

Visit your local delicatessen or supermarket in search of special foods to create either a Spanish or Italian theme. Look for items such as pickled garlic, breads and breadsticks, marinated artichoke hearts, olives, peperoncini, salted almonds, interesting cheeses, salamis, and air-dried hams, such as Serrano or prosciutto. Serve them presented on a platter.

Warm spicy almonds

Put 1 cup Spanish or another variety of whole blanched almonds in a frying pan with 1 tablespoon olive oil and 1 teaspoon smoky paprika or chili powder. Pan-fry until completely golden. Serve immediately in small bowls.

Tomato and feta skewers

To make 20 skewers, cut a piece of feta cheese into 1-in (2.5-cm) cubes and chop 10 cherry tomatoes in half. Feed 1 cube of feta and a tomato half onto each skewer. In a bowl, mix 1 teaspoon crushed fennel seeds, 1 tablespoon grated lemon rind, a pinch of crushed chili pepper, and 1 tablespoon extra-virgin olive oil. Place the skewers in a dish, season with salt and pepper, pour on the marinade mixture, and leave for an hour. Serve the skewers on a platter.

Selection of sushi

Visit your local supermarket or a specialty shop and buy the freshest sushi available. Serve the selection of fish and rolls with chopsticks, wasabi paste, soy dipping sauce, and perhaps a few glasses of sake.

Gorgonzola crostini with red onion

Toast some sliced sourdough or French bread, then spread a thick slice of Gorgonzola over each slice. Top with a couple of thinly sliced rings of red onion and a sprinkling of balsamic vinegar. Season with black pepper and serve.

Pistachios or Japanese rice-coated peanuts

Visit your local supermarket or a specialty shop to buy fresh, unshelled pistachios, Japanese rice-coated peanuts, or any other of your favorite nuts, and serve them in small bowls.

Prosciutto-wrapped melon

Prosciutto-wrapped melon

Cut a cantaloupe, or any other sweet melon, into 1-in (2.5-cm) chunks. Slice some prosciutto, or Serrano ham, into small strips. Wrap a strip of ham around each chunk of melon and secure it with a toothpick or skewer.

Parmesan crisps

Freshly grate some Parmesan and arrange it in thin piles, about 2 tablespoons at a time, on a baking sheet lined with parchment paper. Bake for 7 minutes at 400°F (200°C). Remove from the oven and let sit for 1 minute, then remove with a metal spatula to a cooling rack.

Steaming hot or refreshingly chilled, soups offer comfort and joy. They are an excellent showcase for the many delicious vegetables and aromatic herbs and spices available. Don't be shy with embellishments: Croutons, dumplings, and pomegranate seeds can be savored with each mouthful.

Soups

Creamy celery and fennel soup
with chilled grapes

This is a wonderfully refreshing and satisfying soup. The sweet, plump grapes enliven the velvety texture with their revitalizing freshness and purple color.

1 Heat the butter and olive oil in a large saucepan over medium heat. Add the fennel, onion, celery, fennel seed, celery seed, garlic, salt and pepper, and sauté, stirring occasionally, for about 10 minutes, until softened. Add the white wine, lemon juice, and stock and simmer for 20 minutes. Stir in the half-and-half and continue to cook gently for an additional 5 minutes.

2 Pour the mixture into a blender or food processor and puree. Serve it in small cups, teacups, or small glasses, garnished with grapes and chives.

Prepare ahead

The soup can be made 2 days in advance, covered, refrigerated, and reheated before serving. Alternatively, it may be frozen for up to 4 weeks.

INGREDIENTS

1 tbsp butter

2 tbsp olive oil

2 fennel bulbs, cored, sliced, and chopped

1 medium-sized yellow onion, finely chopped

1 celery heart, sliced

½ tsp fennel seeds, crushed

¼ tsp celery seed

2 garlic cloves, finely chopped

½ tsp each salt and pepper

¾ cup white wine

Juice of ½ lemon

1⅔ cups chicken or vegetable stock

¼ cup half-and-half

1 large handful purple seedless grapes, halved

Chopped chives, to garnish (*optional*)

Preparation time 25 minutes
Cooking time 35 minutes
Makes 8 small cups or 4 bowls

BUY AND ARRANGE	PARTNER WITH
Frisee with quail's eggs (*see p93*) • smoked salmon blinis (*see p148*) • lemon curd spread on toasted brioche (*see p214*)	Baby beets and bresaola (*see p168*) • seared beef carpaccio (*see p128*) • baby clams (*see p136*)

Chili gazpacho
with sourdough croutons

Nothing is as easy, healthy, and refreshing as gazpacho. If you can't find an ancho chili, use any other dried red chili or a teaspoon of Tabasco sauce.

1 Soak the ancho chili pepper in boiling water for 15 minutes. Drain, place in the food processor or blender with the water, and puree. Reserve 1 tablespoon of the mixture and transfer the rest to a jar. Float a little oil over the top to cover, and seal the jar. Store the jar for use another time.

2 Place the tomatoes, onion, cucumber, and peppers in a large bowl. Add the ancho chili puree, garlic, bread, olive oil, stock, vinegar, spices, salt, and pepper. Stir to combine thoroughly. Transfer to a food processor or blender and process to a smooth puree. If you want a finer texture, sieve the mixture. Chill for at least 4 hours or overnight.

3 Divide the soup between 8 cups or 4 bowls, top with the sourdough croutons, and serve cold.

Prepare ahead
The soup can be made the night before, and tastes much better that way.

INGREDIENTS

1 dried ancho chili pepper, deseeded and stem removed

2 tbsp water

3 tbsp olive oil, plus a little to top the puree

1 lb (500 g) ripe plum tomatoes, coarsely chopped

1 small red onion, coarsely chopped

1 small cucumber, coarsely chopped

½ large red pepper, deseeded and coarsely chopped

½ yellow pepper, deseeded and coarsely chopped

1 garlic clove, crushed

2 slices white bread, crusts removed and torn into chunks

1 cup cold chicken stock

2 tbsp sherry vinegar

½ tsp pimenton (smoked paprika)

1 tsp cumin seed, toasted

½ tsp each salt and pepper

1 recipe sourdough croutons (see three-tomato salad, p86), to serve

Preparation time 25 minutes, plus 4 hours or overnight chilling time

Makes 8 small cups or 4 bowls

BUY AND ARRANGE	PARTNER WITH
Salsa with tortilla chips (see p70) • baby lettuce with walnut oil and sherry vinegar (see p92) • ice cream with sweet sherry (see p214)	Beef and sweet potato skewers (see p114) • crispy chorizo quesadillas (see p186) • crab and gruyére nachos (see p142)

Mushroom and chestnut soup
with truffle oil

Chestnuts have a true affinity for mushrooms. If you are feeling extravagant, drizzle on some truffle oil when ready to serve.

1 Soak the porcini mushrooms in 2 cups of boiling water for 15 minutes. Put the olive oil in a medium-sized saucepan, heat to medium-high, and add the onion, salt, and pepper. Sauté for 4 minutes, then add the garlic. Reduce the heat to medium and sauté for 2 minutes. Add the fresh mushrooms and chestnuts, and sauté for an additional minute before adding the stock.

2 Drain the porcini, reserving the liquid. Rinse, chop finely, and add to the soup. Strain the liquid through paper towels to catch any remaining grit or dirt, pour the strained liquid into the soup, and cook for 20 minutes. Stir in the cream and lemon juice. Season to taste, then transfer to a blender and puree. Return to the saucepan to warm through. Serve in cups or bowls, garnished with chopped chives and a drizzle of truffle oil, if using.

Prepare ahead

The soup can be made 2 days before, refrigerated and reheated. It may also be frozen for up to 4 weeks.

INGREDIENTS

1 oz (30 g) dried porcini mushrooms

6 tbsp olive oil

1 yellow onion, finely diced

½ tsp each salt and pepper

2 garlic cloves, finely chopped

1 lb (500 g) white button or Portobello mushrooms, stems trimmed and finely chopped

3½ oz (100 g) vacuum-packed chestnuts, finely chopped

2½ cups chicken or vegetable stock

½ cup half-and-half

Juice of ½ lemon

Chives, chopped, for garnish

Truffle oil, to garnish (*optional*)

Preparation time 20 minutes
Cooking time 28 minutes
Makes 8 small cups or 4 bowls

BUY AND ARRANGE	PARTNER WITH
Shaved celery salad (*see p92*) • white bean dip (*see p71*) • ice cream with sweet sherry (*see p214*)	Spiced goat cheese balls (*see p59*) • spinach and peppered pear salad (*see p84*) • roasted shrimp and tomatoes (*see p145*)

Orange and beet soup
with iced yogurt cubes

This colorful soup will win over anyone with a beet aversion. If you haven't prepared the ice cubes, simply stir in a spoonful of yogurt before serving.

1 Put the yogurt in a bowl and stir in half of the chives. Spoon the mixture into an ice-cube tray and place in the freezer until frozen.

2 Put the beets in a saucepan, cover with water, and boil for 45 minutes to 1 hour, or until easily pierced with a knife. When cool enough to handle, remove the skins, chop roughly, and set aside.

3 Meanwhile, heat the olive oil over medium heat in a medium-sized saucepan and add the onion, garlic, thyme, salt, and pepper. Sauté for 10 minutes, then add the beets, vinegar, zest, orange juice, and stock. Simmer for 10 minutes, then transfer to a blender or food processor and puree.

4 Stir in the half-and-half and adjust the seasoning. Transfer to cups or bowls, drop in the iced yogurt cubes, and sprinkle with the remaining chives.

Prepare ahead

The soup can be made the day before and refrigerated, or frozen for up to 3 weeks.

INGREDIENTS

1 cup plain natural yogurt

Small bunch of chives, chopped

1 lb (500 g) small beets, scrubbed and leaves trimmed

6 tbsp olive oil

1 onion, chopped

2 garlic cloves, finely chopped

1 tbsp chopped fresh thyme

½ tsp each salt and pepper, plus more as needed

1 tsp balsamic vinegar

1 tbsp grated orange zest

Juice of ½ orange

4 cups chicken or vegetable stock

3 tbsp half-and-half

Preparation time 15 minutes
Cooking time 1 hour
Makes 8 small cups or 4 bowls

BUY AND ARRANGE

Prosciutto-wrapped melon (*see p31*) • crushed feta dip (*see p70*) • roasted new potatoes with smoky paprika (*see p173*)

PARTNER WITH

Pan-fried halloumi salad (*see p82*) • smoky eggplant puree (*see p64*) • fried artichokes, Roman style (*see p12*)

Saffron coconut soup
with shrimp dumplings

Tom yum paste is made from ingredients such as galangal, lemongrass, chili pepper, garlic, and lime, and it tastes better than any homemade version.

1 To make the dumplings, place the ginger, garlic, shallots, and cilantro in a food processor and process until finely chopped. Add the shrimp, egg white, corn starch, salt and pepper, and process to combine thoroughly. Rub oil over your hands to prevent sticking, roll the mixture into ½-in (1-cm) balls, and place in the refrigerator.

2 Place the coconut milk in a medium-sized saucepan and heat gently. Add the tom yum paste, lime juice, and saffron, stir well, bring to a gentle boil, then reduce the heat. Just before serving, add the dumplings and watercress. As soon as the dumplings float to the top, remove the soup from the heat and pour into cups, glasses, or teacups. Sprinkle with mint and cilantro, and serve.

Prepare ahead
The soup can be made the day before and refrigerated. The dumplings can be prepared on the morning of serving, then covered and refrigerated. Alternatively, make them up to 2 weeks ahead, place in an airtight container, and freeze.

INGREDIENTS

2 x 14-oz (400-ml) cans coconut milk

1 tbsp instant tom yum paste or 1 tom yum stock cube

Juice of ½ lime

Small pinch saffron threads, crushed

1 large bunch watercress, roughly chopped

Small handful fresh mint, to garnish

Small handful fresh cilantro, to garnish

Dumplings
1 tsp grated fresh root ginger

½ garlic clove, chopped

2 shallots, sliced

1 tsp fresh chopped cilantro

8 oz (225 g) raw peeled shrimp

1 egg white

1 tsp corn starch

¼ tsp each salt and pepper

Olive oil, for shaping—see method

Preparation time 15 minutes
Cooking time 10 minutes
Makes 8 small servings

BUY AND ARRANGE	PARTNER WITH
Selection of sushi (see p31) • Japanese rice-coated peanuts (see p31) • fresh unpeeled lychees (see p215)	Glass noodle salad (see p76) • seafood spring rolls (see p176) • raspberry meringues (see p208)

Yellow lentil soup
with prunes, apricots, and pomegranates

Dried fruit lends depth to the lentils, and together with the pomegranate molasses this is a glorious sweet and sour soup. In summer, blend in some yogurt and serve chilled.

1 Heat the oil over medium-high heat in a large saucepan. Add the onions, carrots, garlic, ginger, salt, and pepper, and sauté for about 10 minutes, until soft. Add the dried fruit, cumin, cardamom, cloves, and cinnamon. Sauté for a few minutes before adding the stock. Stir in the lentils and cook, covered, for about 1 hour, until the lentils are very soft.

2 Stir in the pomegranate molasses and fresh herbs, and taste for seasoning. Serve in small cups or mugs, garnished with pomegranate seeds and cilantro sprigs. The soup may be pureed for a smoother texture, if desired.

Prepare ahead

The soup may be made 2 days in advance, and refrigerated, or frozen for up to 4 weeks.

INGREDIENTS

3 tbsp olive oil

2 onions, chopped

2 carrots, finely chopped

3 garlic cloves, finely chopped

1-in (2.5-cm) piece fresh ginger root, grated

½ tsp salt

½ tsp pepper

6 pitted prunes, roughly chopped

8 dried apricots, roughly chopped

1 tsp ground cumin

¼ tsp ground cardamom

¼ tsp ground cloves

2 cinnamon sticks

4 cups chicken or vegetable stock

2¼ cups yellow or red lentils

2 tbsp pomegranate molasses or juice of 1 lemon

Small handful of mint leaves, chopped

Small handful cilantro, chopped, plus sprigs to garnish

Pomegranate seeds, to garnish

Preparation time 20 minutes
Cooking time 1¼ hours
Serves 8 small cups or 4 bowls

BUY AND ARRANGE	PARTNER WITH
Lebanese salad plate (see p93) • hummus with smoked paprika (see p70) • oranges with rose water (see p214)	Spinach and yogurt dip (see p66) • saffron chicken skewers (see p98) • cardamom poached apricots (see p211)

Red curry pumpkin soup
with crispy fried shallots

Thai red curry paste is very useful as a quick-fix for meals and adds real spice to this soup. The fried shallots provide a spirited counterpoint to the richness of the pumpkin.

1   Heat 2 tablespoons of oil over medium-high heat in a medium-sized saucepan, add the garlic, and fry until browned. Stir in the curry paste, fry for 3 minutes, stirring constantly, then pour in the coconut milk. Stir in the fish sauce, lime zest and juice, sugar, and stock. Simmer for 2 minutes. Reduce the heat, add the pumpkin, and cook for an additional 8–10 minutes, or until soft.

2   Place the flour in a small bowl, add the shallots, and toss to coat. Remove the shallots and shake off the excess flour. Pour the remaining oil into a wok or a small, heavy-bottomed saucepan. Heat until a small piece of bread, dropped in, sizzles immediately. Add the shallots and fry for 1–2 minutes, until golden. Drain on paper towels and sprinkle with salt.

3   Serve the warm soup in cups or bowls, sprinkled with the shallots and the cilantro sprigs.

Prepare ahead

The soup can be made the day before and refrigerated. If doing this, undercook the pumpkin so that it doesn't become mushy when reheating. The soup may also be frozen for up to 4 weeks. The fried shallots can be prepared 3 hours in advance and kept in an airtight container. Reheat for 5 minutes in an oven preheated to 400°F (200°C).

INGREDIENTS

2 tbsp peanut or vegetable oil, plus 2½ cups for frying

1 garlic clove, chopped

4 tbsp good-quality Thai red curry paste

1⅔ cups coconut milk

1 tbsp fish sauce

Zest and juice of 1 lime

1 tbsp superfine sugar

½ cup chicken stock

1-lb (500-g) pumpkin, deseeded and cut into 1-in (2.5-cm) pieces

4 tbsp all-purpose flour

5 shallots, sliced very thinly

Salt, to taste

A few sprigs of cilantro, to garnish

Preparation time 10 minutes
Cooking time 18 minutes
Makes 8 small cups or 4 bowls

BUY AND ARRANGE

Watercress salad with spring onion (see p93) • shrimp and cucumber skewers (see p149) • freshly sliced kiwi (see p215)

PARTNER WITH

Thai corn fritters (see p26) • crispy pork (see p119) • avocado crostini (see p164)

Meatball and pecorino soup
with greens and caramelized onion

These tiny meatballs combine with the pungent greens, caramelized onion, and sharp pecorino cheese, creating a satisfying soup. Pork can easily be used in place of the veal.

1 To make the soup, heat the oil over medium-high heat in a heavy-bottomed, medium-sized saucepan. Add the onion, season with salt and pepper, and fry for about 10 minutes until the onions are golden-brown and caramelized. Remove from the heat and set aside.

2 Meanwhile, bring a large saucepan of salted water to a boil. Add the chopped kale and cook for about 4 minutes, making sure it is cooked but still firm. Drain, rinse in cold water, and set aside.

3 To make the meatballs, place the bread in a medium-sized bowl, spoon the milk over to soften, and break up the bread with your fingers. Add the remaining meatball ingredients and mix well. Using floured hands, roll the mixture into ½-in (1-cm) balls. Heat a small amount of olive oil in a nonstick frying pan, add the meatballs, and fry. Turn regularly, until browned and crisp.

4 Add the kale, stock, and meatballs to the onions in the saucepan, and heat through. Ladle into cups or bowls, and sprinkle with the pecorino. Serve with some small slices of toast, if using.

Prepare ahead
The onions can be caramelized 2 days in advance. The soup may also be frozen for up to 4 weeks.

INGREDIENTS

3 tbsp olive oil

2 yellow onions, thinly sliced

Salt and freshly ground black pepper, to taste

8 oz (225 g) curly kale, chopped

3 cups chicken stock

Pecorino cheese, shaved into slivers, for garnishing

Toasted bread, to serve (*optional*)

Meatballs

1 slice white bread

2 tbsp milk

8 oz (250 g) minced veal or pork

½ garlic clove, finely chopped

2 tbsp Parmesan

1 egg yolk, beaten

1 tsp salt

2 tbsp finely chopped flat-leaf parsley

Flour, to dust hands

1 tbsp olive oil, for frying

Preparation 20 minutes
Cooking time 20 minutes
Makes 8 small cups or 4 bowls

BUY AND ARRANGE	PARTNER WITH
Radicchio, orange, and arugula salad (*see p92*) • biscotti, mascarpone, and dessert wine (*see p215*)	Serrano-rolled asparagus (*see p152*) • bagna cauda dip (*see p54*) • chocolate Frangelico pudding (*see p200*)

Tomato and ginger soup
with spiced oil

This recipe is based on a restorative soup, called rasam in India, that is said to be the equivalent of chicken soup. Use the juice of two lemons instead of tamarind if necessary.

1 Place the tomatoes, garlic, and ginger in a blender or food processor, and blend for 1 minute or until smooth. Pour into a large saucepan, and add the tamarind liquid, stock, cilantro, jalapeños, sugar, turmeric, salt, and pepper. Bring the mixture to a boil, reduce the heat to medium, and cook for 15 minutes.

2 Meanwhile, heat the oil in a small frying pan and add the mustard seeds. When they begin to pop, add the cumin, and asafoetida, if using. Fry for 1 minute, stirring, then remove from the heat.

3 Divide the soup between 8 cups or 6 bowls. Spoon the spiced oil mixture over the top and garnish with the cilantro sprigs.

Prepare ahead
The soup can be made the day before and refrigerated. Alternatively, it may be frozen for up to 4 weeks.

INGREDIENTS

15 ripe plum or vine-ripened tomatoes, chopped

6 garlic cloves

2-in (5-cm) piece fresh ginger root, peeled and sliced

1 cup tamarind liquid or puree

1 cup chicken or vegetable stock

Medium-sized bunch cilantro, finely chopped, plus sprigs to garnish

2 fresh jalapeños, deseeded and slit lengthwise

1½ tbsp soft light brown sugar

1 tsp turmeric powder

1 tsp salt

½ tsp ground black pepper

5 tbsp vegetable oil

2 tsp mustard seeds

1 tsp cumin seeds

Pinch of asafoetida (*optional*)

Preparation time 20 minutes
Cooking time 20 minutes
Makes 8 small cups or 6 bowls

BUY AND ARRANGE	PARTNER WITH
Selection of chutneys and pickles (*see p70*) • raita with naan bread (*see p71*) • freshly sliced watermelon (*see p215*)	Pea and shrimp samosas (*see p194*) • tandoori chicken thighs (*see p130*) • chocolate cupcakes (*see p202*)

There is something beguiling about dipping; perhaps it's the absence of cutlery, the creamy textures, and the idea of sharing food with friends. From the garlicky bagna cauda and smoky black bean, to the tangy garbanzo and chili pepper, there is a dip here to suit every taste.

Dips

Bagna cauda dip
with crudities and quail's eggs

If you have a fondue pot, keep the sauce warm in it while serving. The untrimmed tops of the carrots, radishes, and tomatoes make natural handles.

1 To make the dip, pound the garlic and anchovies with a mortar and pestle until smooth, then transfer to a small saucepan. Add the butter and oil and simmer over medium heat for 4 minutes or until melted, stirring occasionally. Stir in the lemon zest and juice, parsley, and chili pepper. Keep warm over very low heat until ready to serve.

2 Prepare your chosen selection of vegetables. Hard-boil the eggs, if using, and peel once cooled. Serve with the dip.

Prepare ahead
The bagna cauda can be made in the morning of serving day, covered and refrigerated, then gently reheated at the last minute. The vegetables can be trimmed and cut the day before, and kept in the refrigerator in an airtight container or bag.

INGREDIENTS

3 garlic cloves, finely chopped

4 large anchovies, packed in olive oil, rinsed and chopped

1 stick (½ cup) unsalted butter

½ cup extra-virgin olive oil

1 tsp grated lemon zest

3 tsp lemon juice

2 tbsp finely chopped flat-leaf parsley

½ tsp crushed dried chili pepper

To serve

Baby carrots

Radishes

Radicchio or treviso leaves

Red pepper, thinly sliced

Cherry tomatoes on the vine

Cucumber wedges

Celery hearts with leaves, cut into batons

8 quail's eggs, boiled and peeled, served with toothpicks or skewers

Sourdough bread, toasted

Preparation time 20 minutes

Makes about 8 servings

BUY AND ARRANGE	PARTNER WITH
Spice-dusted shrimp (see p148) • Italian deli plate (see p30) • marinated olives with oranges (see p30)	Artichoke puff pastry bites (see p196) • sage and lemon meatballs (see p131) • three-tomato salad (see p86)

Romesco dip
with roasted baby potatoes

If you can't find ancho chili peppers, any other large dried chili pepper will do. Try pimenton in place of the paprika for a smokier flavor.

1 Preheat the oven to 400°F (200°C). Place the potatoes on a large, nonstick baking sheet. Drizzle with 2 tablespoons of olive oil and sprinkle with half of the salt and pepper. Roast for 20–30 minutes, until golden and crisp. Remove and set aside.

2 To make the dip, meanwhile, preheat the broiler to high. Place the tomatoes under the broiler and cook until blackened. When cool enough, remove and discard the skins, and set aside. Place the garlic in a nonstick sauté pan and dry-fry over meidum-high heat, stirring, until blackened on all sides. Remove and discard the skins when cool. Set aside. In the same pan, toast the almonds and hazelnuts, stirring, until golden. Set aside.

3 Put the red wine vinegar and water in a saucepan, bring to a boil, remove from the heat, and add the chili peppers. Soak for 10–15 minutes, until softened. Remove the peppers and discard the liquid.

4 Transfer the tomatoes, chili peppers, garlic, and nuts to a food processor, along with the bread, paprika, sherry vinegar, ¼ cup olive oil, and remaining salt and pepper. Puree, leaving the nuts slightly chunky. Serve the dip with the potatoes and garnished with the flat-leaf parsley.

Prepare ahead
The dip can be prepared 2 days ahead and refrigerated. The potatoes may be slightly under-roasted 4 hours ahead, then roasted for 5–6 minutes in an oven preheated to 400°F (200°C).

INGREDIENTS

1½ lb (750 g) baby potatoes

2 tbsp extra-virgin olive oil, plus ¼ cup

1 tsp each sea salt and pepper

4 large or 6 small plum tomatoes, halved

5 garlic cloves, in their skins

15 blanched almonds

15 blanched hazelnuts

¼ cup red wine vinegar

¾ cup water

2 dried ancho chili peppers, deseeded and stems removed

1 slice white bread, toasted

1 tsp paprika or pimenton

3 tbsp sherry vinegar

Fresh flat-leaf parsley, to garnish

Preparation time 25 minutes
Cooking time 30 minutes
Makes 8 servings

BUY AND ARRANGE

Pan-fried chorizo (see p149) • tomato and feta skewers (see p31) • marinated fresh anchovies (see p30)

PARTNER WITH

Beef and sweet potato skewers (see p114) • Serrano-rolled asparagus (see p152) • zucchini ribbon rolls (see p160)

Smoky black bean dip
with chili peppers and honey

This dip is incredibly healthy, so you don't have to hold back on how much you eat. Instead of the chipotle, you can use another chili pepper or a teaspoon of Tabasco.

1　If using canned beans, drain and set aside. If using soaked dried beans, drain, place in a medium-sized saucepan, and cover with water. Boil for about 45 minutes, until just tender. Drain.

2　Meanwhile, heat the olive oil in a sauté pan. Add the onion, red pepper, chipotle pepper, and garlic. Sauté for 4 minutes. Add the beans, vinegar, honey, chili powder, cumin, salt, and pepper. Simmer over low heat for about 5 minutes, stirring occasionally.

3　Puree the mixture in a food processor. Add extra honey, cider vinegar, or salt, according to taste. The beans will cook and absorb flavors differently each time you prepare them. If desired, serve with salted tortilla chips and fruit salsa.

Prepare ahead
The dip can be made a week in advance and kept refrigerated.

INGREDIENTS

⅔ cup dried black beans, soaked overnight, or 8 oz (250 g) canned black beans, drained

3 tbsp olive oil

1 onion, chopped

1 red pepper, chopped

1 chipotle pepper, deseeded and chopped

3 cloves garlic, chopped

½ cup cider vinegar

4 tbsp honey

1 tsp each chili powder and ground cumin

1 tbsp sea salt

Freshly cracked pepper

Tortilla chips and fruit salsa (see p70), to serve (optional)

Preparation time 30 minutes
Cooking time 45 minutes
Makes about 8 servings

BUY AND ARRANGE

Watermelon and feta salad (see p93) • pan-fried chorizo (see p149) • spice-dusted shrimp (see p148)

PARTNER WITH

Crab and Gruyère nachos (see p142) • soft-shell steak tacos (see p178) • grilled butterfly shrimp (see p141)

Goat cheese balls
rolled in spices

This dish is still impressive without the caramelized garlic, so if you're short on time, make the balls with just the goat cheese and spices.

1 To caramelize the garlic, place the cloves in a small saucepan, cover with water, and boil for 3 minutes. Drain, peel, and slice each clove into 3 pieces.

2 Heat the olive oil in a saucepan over low heat, add the garlic, and lightly brown. Drain off the oil, add the vinegar, rosemary, salt, pepper, and sugar, and cook for 3 minutes, until the liquid is reduced to a thick syrup. Pour onto a plate and leave to cool.

3 In a small bowl, mash the goat cheese. Stir in the salt, pepper, and caramelized garlic. Mix well and roll into 1-in (2.5-cm) balls.

4 Place the spices in separate bowls. Roll each ball in a different spice to coat. Refrigerate for 30 minutes. Serve at room temperature with thin crackers or garlic crostini.

Prepare ahead
The cheese balls can be prepared the day before and refrigerated.

INGREDIENTS

1 small head garlic, unpeeled, cloves separated

3 tbsp olive oil

2 tbsp white wine vinegar

1 tsp finely chopped rosemary

Pinch each of salt, pepper, and sugar

8 oz (250 g) soft, mild rindless goat cheese

½ tsp each salt and pepper

1 tbsp fennel seeds, crushed

1 tbsp cracked black pepper

1 tbsp crushed pink peppercorns, poppy seeds, or pimento

Thin crackers or garlic crostini, to serve

Preparation time 20 minutes
Cooking time 8 minutes
Makes about 24 balls

BUY AND ARRANGE

Chicory salad (see p93) •
pesto and aioli with grissini
breadsticks (see p70) •
raspberry fool (see p215)

PARTNER WITH

Creamy celery and fennel soup
(see p34) • chunky chopped
salad (see p74) • chocolate
crinkle cookies (see p204)

Colors
- Magenta pink
- Moss green
- Shimmering white
- Soft yellow
- Duck-egg blue

Tableware
- Banana leaves
- Floating candles
- Straw mats
- Simple plates
- Crackle-glazed dipping bowls

Pacific feast

Follow the ring of fire that encircles the highly volcanic area around the Pacific Ocean and you will encounter China, Japan, Indonesia, Thailand, Korea, Vietnam, and Laos—all countries distinguished by lush eating. Pacific Rim cuisine has a vibrant taste characterized by lemongrass, ginger, chili peppers, mint, lime, and soy sauce. While this food gives the impression of being casually made, its composition is sophisticated. Texture is vitally important, providing a satisfying crunch, with an exquisite melange of tastes. In this cooking tradition, each individual flavor is evident yet not dominant.

One of the wonderful aspects of this food is its many sauces, most featuring chili peppers. Some sauces are sticky, made with rice vinegar and sugar, while others comprise simply lime juice and fish sauce. Go easy when using chili peppers—you're seeking taste as well as kick. Keep in mind that the bigger the chili pepper, the milder its heat.

Embellish your table with a few Pacific touches—bowls filled with exotic flowers, candles floating in water, banana leaves, and straw mats. Though Pacific Rim is quintessential summer food, it's refreshing any time, even in deepest winter.

Flavors

- Tangy lime
- Fresh ginger
- Spicy chili peppers
- Cool mint
- Exotic lemongrass

Nibbles

- Five-spice chicken bites (*see p149*)
- Crab and cream cheese dip (*see p71*)
- Rice-coated peanuts (*see p31*)
- Thai shrimp (*see p149*)
- Spicy peanut dip (*see p71*)

Menu

Lemongrass beef skewers with sticky
cucumber and peanut sauce

Seafood spring rolls with sweet chili
pepper and cilantro dipping sauce

Thai corn fritters with sweet chili
pepper and cilantro dipping sauce

Glass noodle salad
with black pepper chicken

Peking seared duck rolls
with plum sauce

Passion fruit trifle
with strawberries and mascarpone

BUY AND ARRANGE

Crab and cream cheese dip
(see p71)

Thai shrimp
(see p149)

Rice-coated peanuts
(see p31)

Lemongrass beef skewers
(see p104)

Seafood spring rolls
(see p176)

Thai corn fritters
(see p26)

Glass noodle salad
(see p76)

Peking seared duck rolls
(see p180)

Passion fruit trifle
(see p206)

Two days before
- Marinate lemongrass beef
- Marinate Peking duck
- Marinate black pepper chicken
- Make sweet chili pepper and
  cilantro sauce

The night before
- Make seafood spring rolls
- Make passion fruit trifles

In the morning
- Assemble beef skewers
- Make sticky cucumber
  dipping sauce
- Broil chicken
- Sear and slice duck

Mango crush

This is a refreshing cocktail to quench your thirst while enjoying chili peppers, spices, and other exotic flavors. Try using watermelon or papaya in place of the mango.

INGREDIENTS

2 large ripe mangoes, peeled and chopped

Juice of 1 lime

2 cups freshly squeezed orange juice

2 tbsp sugar

6 measures of vodka

Ice

Mint sprigs, to garnish

Makes 6 mango crushes

Put the mango, lime, orange juice, sugar, and vodka in a food processor or blender and puree until smooth. Add some ice to 6 glasses and pour the cocktail over it. Garnish with a few mint sprigs.

Two hours before

- Broil and parcook beef skewers
- Make batter for fritters
- Make crab and cream cheese dip, omitting the cilantro and onion
- Assemble glass noodle salad, omitting the herbs
- Make Peking duck rolls

Half- to one hour before

- Fry corn fritters
- Puree mango crush
- Broil and finish cooking beef skewers, rest, then plate
- Plate seafood spring rolls with dipping sauce
- Plate Peking duck rolls

At the last minute

- Reheat corn fritters; plate
- Toss herbs with glass noodle salad; plate
- Finish crab dip with cilantro, onion, and crackers; plate
- Pour mango crush
- Serve passion fruit trifles

Smoky eggplant puree
with crushed coriander and mint

Eggplants are chameleons, changing their flavor and texture depending on the way they are cooked and the other ingredients used. Blackening them over a flame, instead of roasting, imparts a magnificent smoky taste.

1 Pierce the eggplants with a knife in several places. Using tongs, place each eggplant over an open flame on the stove. Turn each one as it blackens, and continue until it is completely charred. The insides will be fine. It can be helpful to place an old cooling rack over the flame so that you can rest the eggplant on it. Alternatively, blacken the eggplants under a broiler or cook on a barbecue gril, but the smokiness will not be quite the same. Place in a colander to drain off any excess liquid. When cool enough to handle, carefully peel off the skin and cut off stalks.

2 While the eggplant is still warm, place the flesh in a food processor. Add the garlic, olive oil, lemon juice, yogurt, pimenton, coriander seed, and mint, and season with salt and pepper. Sprinkle with the chopped onion and cucumber. Serve with pita bread or crudités.

Prepare ahead

The dip can be made 2 hours in advance and refrigerated, then brought to room temperature before serving. Don't add the chopped vegetables until ready to serve.

INGREDIENTS

2 large, firm eggplants

1 garlic clove, finely chopped

¼ cup olive oil

1 tbsp fresh lemon juice

2 tbsp yogurt

½ tsp pimenton

½ tsp coriander seeds, lightly crushed

¼ cup fresh mint, finely chopped

Salt and pepper, to taste

1 small red onion, finely chopped, to garnish

1 small cucumber, finely diced, to garnish

Toasted pita bread or crudités, to serve

Prep time 10 minutes
Cooking time 20 minutes
Makes about 8 servings

BUY AND ARRANGE

Crushed feta dip (*see p70*) • carrots in vinaigrette (*see p173*) • Middle Eastern pastries (*see p214*)

PARTNER WITH

Serrano-wrapped shrimp (*see p108*) • pan-fried halloumi salad (*see p82*) • garbanzo and chili pepper dip (*see p68*)

Spinach and yogurt dip
with caramelized onion

This exotic Persian dip is wonderfully rich because of the slowly caramelized onion, but the yogurt and spinach keep it tasting fresh and healthy.

1   Place the spinach in a covered saucepan with the salt, and heat gently for 2 minutes, until it wilts. Drain and rinse with cold water, then squeeze off any excess water with your hands, until dry.

2   Place the oil in a small frying pan, add the onions and garlic, and sauté slowly for about 20 minutes, until golden brown. It's important to cook until caramelized to bring out the sweet flavor. Remove from heat, set aside, and allow to cool completely.

3   In a mixing bowl, combine the onion mixture, yogurt, and spinach. Season with salt and pepper. Refrigerate, then serve with warm pita bread.

Prepare ahead

Cook the onions and spinach on the morning of the same day you plan to serve to them, but don't mix them with the yogurt until 2 hours before serving.

INGREDIENTS

12 oz (350 g) fresh spinach, chopped

1 tsp salt

2 tbsp olive oil

2 large yellow onions, finely sliced

2 garlic cloves, crushed

1 cup plain, natural full-fat yogurt

Pita bread, to serve

Preparation time 10 minutes
Cooking time 25 minutes
Makes about 8 servings

BUY AND ARRANGE

Piquillo peppers with sherry vinegar (see p172) • baby lettuce with walnut oil and sherry vinegar (see p92)

PARTNER WITH

Saffron feta phyllo triangles (see p182) • cardamom-poached apricots (see p211) • saffron chicken skewers (see p98)

Roasted beet pesto
with Parmesan

This is a very simple dip to make. The earthy roasted beets make this pesto notable not only for its rich purple color but also for its deliciously nutty taste.

1 Preheat the oven to 400°F (200°C). Place the beets on a large piece of foil, drizzle with 1 tablespoon of olive oil, and season with salt and pepper. Wrap tightly in foil, to create an airtight package. Place in the oven for 45 minutes, or until easily pierced with a knife.

2 Remove the skin from the beets and discard. Put the beets in a food processor with the garlic, pine nuts, and ½ teaspoon salt. Puree the mixture until smooth. Add the Parmesan, puree again, then slowly add the remaining oil, still pureeing. Add extra salt, if needed. Serve with garlic crostini or toasted pita bread.

Prepare ahead
The pesto can be made 3 days in advance, covered, and kept in the refrigerator.

INGREDIENTS

2 medium-sized raw beets, halved

Salt and pepper, to taste, plus ½ tsp salt

¼ cup extra-virgin olive oil, plus 1 tbsp

2 garlic cloves, peeled

4 oz (100 g) pine nuts, toasted and cooled

¼ cup Parmesan

Garlic crostini or toasted pita bread, to serve

Preparation time 10 minutes
Cooking time 45 minutes
Makes about 8 servings

BUY AND ARRANGE

Italian deli plate (see p30) • roasted shallots (see p173) • pan-fried chorizo (see p149)

PARTNER WITH

Fried artichokes, Roman style (see p12) • farro salad (see p78) • mini peach and raspberry crisps (see p212)

Garbanzo and pomegranate dip
with pita chips

Garbanzos, salty feta, and tangy pomegranate blend perfectly in this dip. One tablespoon each of lemon juice and honey, mixed, can be used in place of the molasses.

1 Place the garbanzos, olive oil, lemon juice, garlic, and salt in a food processor and process until just crushed. Divide between the pita chips or place in a serving bowl.

2 Sprinkle each pita chip or the bowl of dip with cumin seeds, red onion, mint, cilantro, and chili peppers. Top with the feta cheese. Just before serving, drizzle with pomegranate molasses.

Prepare ahead

The garbanzo mixture can be pureed in the morning of serving day, and the onions chopped and tossed in the lemon juice to prevent discoloring. Fresh herbs and cheese may be sprinkled on 1 hour before serving. The pita chips can be made 3 days ahead and stored in an airtight container.

INGREDIENTS

2 x 14-oz (400-g) cans of garbanzos, drained

⅓ cup extra-virgin olive oil

Juice of 1 lemon

1 clove garlic, peeled and finely chopped

½ tsp salt

1 recipe pita chips (see p217)

1 tsp cumin seeds

1 small red onion, finely chopped

3 tbsp fresh mint leaves, finely chopped

3 tbsp fresh cilantro leaves, finely chopped

2 red chili peppers, deseeded and finely chopped

5 oz (150 g) feta cheese, crumbled

2 tbsp pomegranate molasses

Preparation time 15 minutes
Makes about 8 servings

BUY AND ARRANGE	PARTNER WITH
Pan-fried lamb Merguez sausage (see p149) • spice-dusted shrimp (see p148) • Middle Eastern pastries (see p214)	Cumin lamb skewers (see p112) • Arabian salad (see p88) • strawberries and figs (see p207)

Quick dips, chutneys, and salsas
buy-and-arrange ideas for quick cooking

Introducing store-bought products into your menu shouldn't make you feel as if you are cheating your guests. Instead, it can create a great base on which to build a dish, adding your favorite spices or herbs to add a personal touch. It also allows you time to make other dishes and will leave you feeling calmer as guests arrive.

Hummus with smoked paprika
Buy an 8-oz (225-g) tub of hummus, tip it out onto a plate, and spread it thickly with a knife across the plate. Sprinkle with 1 teaspoon pimenton or toasted cumin seeds and drizzle with 1 teaspoon extra-virgin olive oil. Serve accompanied by cos lettuce leaves or warm flat bread, such as pita, to scoop up the dip.

Fruit salsa
Dice some fresh fruit, such as mango, papaya, or pineapple; enough to make about 2 handfuls. Place the fruit in a bowl with 1 diced small red onion, 1 small handful chopped fresh cilantro, 1 teaspoon Tabasco sauce, and the juice of 1 lime. Season and combine the mixture well. Serve with a variety of corn tortilla chips.

Pesto and aioli with grissini breadsticks, olive oil, and vinegar
Visit your local delicatessen, or the deli section of a supermarket, to buy some fresh pesto, garlic aioli, extra-virgin olive oil, and balsamic vinegar. There are some interesting breadsticks available, such as grissini or sesame-coated. Pour the dips into separate bowls and serve with breadsticks.

Crushed feta dip with lemon juice and cumin
Buy a 7-oz (225-g) pack of feta cheese and crumble it roughly into a bowl. Add 1 tablespoon extra-virgin olive oil, ½ finely chopped small red onion, the zest and juice of 1 lemon, and ½ teaspoon toasted cumin seeds. Combine the mixture together well and serve with fresh crusty bread or carrot batons.

Selection of chutneys and pickles with mini poppadoms
Buy some jars of good-quality lime pickle and mango chutney, and seek out any other Indian-inspired pickles. Serve them in separate bowls with serving spoons and some mini poppadoms or naan bread.

Mexican salsa with tortilla chips
There are some excellent-quality Mexican salsas available in supermarkets. Buy your favorite and, if you wish to give it an extra kick, add a few drops of Tabasco sauce, a squeeze of half a lime, and a small handful of chopped fresh cilantro. Stir in the added ingredients and serve with unsalted tortilla chips.

Crab and cream cheese dip

Spread 4 oz (125 g) cream cheese over a plate with a knife. Sprinkle on a large handful of fresh cooked or canned white crab meat. Drizzle with 2 tablespoons sweet chili pepper dipping sauce and 1 small handful freshly chopped cilantro. Serve with shrimp crackers. Alternatively, arrange the dip on individual shrimp crackers.

Roasted garlic with warm bread

Cut 2 bulbs of garlic in half, drizzle with 1 tablespoon olive oil, and wrap each of the four halves in aluminum foil. Roast them in the oven for 1 hour at 400°F (200°C). Discard the garlic skins and squeeze the warm insides onto slices of fresh bread, preferably a French baguette. Top the bread with soft goat cheese, if desired.

Yogurt and dill dip

In a bowl, blend together some plain yogurt, about 1 cup, with 1 crushed garlic clove, 2 chopped scallions, and a small handful of finely chopped dill. Serve with pita or cucumber cut into batons.

Raita with naan bread

In a bowl, mix together about 1 cup plain yogurt, 1 small diced and deseeded cucumber, 1 diced and deseeded tomato, 1 teaspoon cumin seed, and 1 small handful chopped mint, and season with salt and pepper. Serve with naan bread.

Crab and cream cheese dip on shrimp crackers

Spicy peanut dip

In a small bowl, use a fork to blend together 6 tablespoons chunky peanut butter, 3 tablespoons hoisin sauce, 1 teaspoon chili pepper sauce, and 4 tablespoons water. Transfer the mixture to a serving bowl and provide sugar snap peas as crudités.

White bean dip

Drain a 14-oz (400-g) can of cannellini beans and blend the beans in a food processor with 1 anchovy, 1 clove garlic, juice of half a lemon, 2 tablespoons extra-virgin olive oil, and salt and pepper. Serve with crudités or fresh bread.

Salad is no longer just about leaves. Noodles, grains, and earthy vegetables have now moved into this sphere. To create the dressing, seek out quality vinegars, oils, herbs, and spices. Zesty and downright delicious, these salads bring the promise of flavor and freshness.

Salads

Chunky chopped salad
with a red wine and caper vinaigrette

Recipes for chopped salads are easily transformed; replace any ingredient with your favorite food. Well-drained marinated artichoke hearts can be used in place of palm hearts, if you are unable to locate them.

1 Place all the salad ingredients in a medium-sized bowl.

2 Add all the vinaigrette ingredients to a small, lidded jar. Close the lid, shake well to combine, then pour over the salad. Mix well and serve.

Prepare ahead

The salad can be assembled, without the onion and basil, in the morning of serving day, covered, and refrigerated. The vinaigrette can be made the day before, but don't add until just before serving.

INGREDIENTS

2 red peppers, cut into 1-in (2½-cm) squares

4 oz (125 g) fresh mini mozzarella balls, or 2 large ones, torn into pieces

7 oz (200 g) canned palm hearts, cut into ½-in (1-cm) slices

2 organic eggs or 5 quail's eggs, hard-boiled, peeled, and quartered

4 oz (125 g) Italian salami, such as pepperoni, sliced

3 celery heart stalks with leaves, chopped

1 small red onion, finely diced

1 small bunch of fresh basil leaves, torn

Vinaigrette

2 tbsp red wine vinegar, such as cabernet sauvignon or chianti

3 tbsp extra-virgin olive oil

½ garlic clove, finely chopped

1 tsp capers, rinsed and chopped

½ tsp each salt and pepper

Preparation time 20 minutes

Makes 8 small cups or 4 appetizers

BUY AND ARRANGE	PARTNER WITH
Smoked salmon blinis (see p148) • chocolate mint ice cream sandwiches (see p215) • white bean dip (see p71)	Halloumi and sourdough spiedini (see p106) • zucchini ribbon rolls (see p160) • chocolate crinkle cookies (see p204)

Glass noodle salad
with black pepper chicken

For a variation on this savory salad, try substituting very fine rice noodles in place of the cellophane noodles. Rice noodles will look more opaque but still taste terrific.

1 To make the marinade, grind together the garlic, cilantro, chili pepper, and black pepper in a food processor or with a mortar and pestle. Add the sesame oil, fish sauce, and honey. Place the chicken in a bowl, coat with the marinade, and leave for at least 30 minutes.

2 Remove the chicken from the marinade and pan-fry over medium-high heat without any fat, or cook under the broiler or on a grill, until very crispy and blackened on the edges. Chop into pieces.

3 Soak the noodles in boiling water for 5 minutes, or until al dente. Drain, rinse in cold water, then pat dry. Cut the noodles in half with scissors and place in a bowl with the onion and herbs.

4 For the dressing, pound the garlic, chili peppers, sugar, and ginger into a paste with a mortar and pestle. Stir in the lime juice and fish sauce. Pour over the salad and mix well. Arrange in bowls, top with chicken, and sprinkle with any leftover herbs and peanuts.

Prepare ahead

The chicken may be left to marinate overnight in the refrigerator. The salad can be made 2 hours before serving, but add the herbs just before serving so that they keep their green color.

BUY AND ARRANGE	PARTNER WITH
Asian cucumber salad (see p93) • selection of sushi (see p30) • fresh unpeeled lychees (see p215)	Seafood spring rolls (see p176) • five-spice hoisin ribs (see p132) • miso halibut bites (see p140)

INGREDIENTS

1 garlic clove, peeled

Small handful cilantro stems, finely chopped

1 tsp crushed dried chili pepper or fresh red chili pepper

1 tbsp freshly ground black pepper

2 tbsp sesame oil

2 tbsp fish sauce

1 tbsp honey

6 boneless, skinless chicken thighs (about 1 lb/500 g)

5 oz (150 g) cellophane noodles (mung bean or glass noodles)

1 medium-sized red onion, finely sliced in half-moons

Large mixed handful of fresh mint, cilantro, and basil leaves (Thai if possible)

Crushed roasted peanuts, to garnish

Dressing

1 garlic clove, minced

½ medium red chili pepper, seeded and finely chopped

2 tbsp soft light brown sugar

1 tbsp grated fresh ginger root

Juice of 3 limes

2 tbsp fish sauce

Preparation and cooking time
30 minutes, plus 30 minutes marinating time

Makes 8 small salads

Farro salad
with anchovy, mint, and pecorino

Farro is a chewy-textured wheat grain that is often called spelt. Risotto rice can be used in its place. It should be well-rinsed and cooked al dente.

1 Preheat the oven to 350°F (180°C). Drain the farro, place in a saucepan of salted water, and boil for 30 minutes, or until tender but not mushy. Meanwhile, place the tomatoes on a nonstick baking tray, drizzle with the oil, and season with salt and pepper. Bake for 20 minutes, then remove from the oven and leave to cool.

2 Place the onion in a large mixing bowl with the lemon juice and leave for 10 minutes to soften the flavor.

3 To make the dressing, heat the oil over medium heat in a sauté pan, add the anchovy and garlic, and brown lightly. As soon as the garlic has colored, add the vinegar, honey, salt, and pepper. Stir well until incorporated. Remove from the heat.

4 Drain the farro and stir it into the diced onion. Add the celery, pecorino, raisins, and roasted tomatoes. Pour into the dressing, mix well, and stir in the herbs. Serve in individual bowls.

Prepare ahead

The dressed salad will keep for 2 hours, but may need a little extra olive oil or vinegar if it dries out. To retain their green color, the herbs should be added just before serving.

INGREDIENTS

1¾ cups farro, soaked for 1 hour in cold water

8 oz (250 g) baby plum or cherry tomatoes, halved

2 tbsp olive oil

½ tsp each salt and pepper

1 red onion, finely diced

Juice of ½ lemon

3 stalks of celery heart, finely sliced

½ cup coarsely grated pecorino cheese

4 tbsp raisins, soaked in warm water for 10 minutes

Small handful each mint, basil, parsley leaves, roughly chopped

Dressing

6 tbsp extra-virgin olive oil

1 anchovy, rinsed and chopped

1 garlic clove, finely chopped

4 tbsp red wine vinegar

1 tsp honey

½ tsp each salt and pepper

Preparation time 30 minutes
Cooking time 30 minutes
Makes 8 small cups of salad or 4 appetizers

BUY AND ARRANGE	PARTNER WITH
Marinated anchovies (*see p30*) • marinated olives (*see p30*) • lemon curd spread on toasted brioche (*see p214*)	Fried artichokes (*see p12*) • mushroom and chestnut soup (*see p38*) • smoky eggplant puree (*see p64*)

Grilled eggplant salad
with pomegranate dressing

Pomegranate molasses is the concentrated juice of the seeds. Use one teaspoon of lemon juice or red wine vinegar mixed with one teaspoon of honey in its place, if you wish.

1 Preheat the broiler to high. Place the peppers skin side up on a nonstick baking sheet. Place under the broiler, cook until blackened, then transfer to a plastic bag, seal, and allow to steam for 5 minutes. When cool enough, peel off the skins and discard, and set the flesh aside.

2 Brush the eggplant with the oil, sprinkle with the cinnamon, and season to taste with salt and pepper. Cook under the broiler until crispy on both sides.

3 To make the dressing, place all of the ingredients in a lidded jar, close it, and shake to combine thoroughly.

4 Arrange the eggplant and pepper on individual plates. Sprinkle with the onion, feta, and cumin seeds. Spoon on the dressing, garnish with the mint, and serve immediately.

Prepare ahead

The salad and dressing can be made in the morning of serving day, but add the feta and onions just before serving. The onions can be chopped and soaked in lemon juice 2 hours ahead.

INGREDIENTS

2 red peppers, quartered, seeds and stem removed

3-4 small eggplants, sliced lengthwise into 1-in (2.5-cm) strips

6 tbsp extra virgin olive oil

½ tsp ground cinnamon

Salt and freshly ground black pepper

1 small red onion, sliced into half-moons

7 oz (200 g) feta cheese, drained and cut into ½-in (1-cm) slices

1 tsp cumin seeds, toasted in a dry pan

Small bunch of mint leaves, roughly chopped, to garnish

Dressing

1 small garlic clove, crushed

Juice of 1 lemon

2 tsp pomegranate molasses

⅓ cup extra-virgin olive oil

1 tsp each salt and pepper

Preparation time 30 minutes
Cooking time 15 minutes
Makes 8 small salads or 4 appetizers

BUY AND ARRANGE	PARTNER WITH
Yogurt and dill dip (see p71) • spice-dusted shrimp (see p148) • oranges with rose water (see p214)	Cumin lamb skewers (see p112) • saffron feta phyllo triangles (see p182) • cardamom-poached apricots (see p211)

Pan-fried halloumi salad
with olive and lemon dressing

Halloumi is a hard Cypriot cheese made from goat and sheep milk. Golden and soft when pan-fried, its salty flavor is balanced by a lemon olive dressing. If you can't find halloumi in your supermarket, you can replace it with mozzarella or order it online.

1 Put all the dressing ingredients in a small bowl, mix together, and set aside. Cut off the peel from the oranges, removing the white pith at the same time. Separate the segments by cutting between the inner membranes with a small serrated knife.

2 Cut the halloumi (or mozzarella) into 16 pieces approximately ½ in (1 cm) thick and 1¼ in (3 cm) by 1¼ in (3 cm) square. Dust them with the flour and season with salt and pepper. Heat the olive oil over medium-high heat in a frying pan until very hot. Add the cheese to the pan in stages, and fry until colored and crispy on both sides. Add more oil if the pan becomes too dry.

3 Arrange small stacks of cheese and orange, then drizzle on the dressing and sprinkle with parsley. Alternatively, scatter the cheese and orange on a serving dish with the dressing and parsley.

Prepare ahead

The dressing can be made the day before. The oranges can be segmented and refrigerated on the morning you plan to serve it The cheese can be pan-fried 1 hour before serving, then reheated or served at room temperature.

INGREDIENTS

2 blood or navel oranges

1 lb (450 g) halloumi, drained

1 cup flour

Salt and pepper, to taste

4 tbsp olive oil

Small bunch flat-leaf parsley, chopped

Dressing

3 tbsp extra-virgin olive oil

10 mild black olives, pitted and finely chopped

Medium bunch flat-leaf parsley, finely chopped

1 tsp capers, rinsed and chopped

½ preserved lemon, rind only, rinsed and finely chopped

2 tsp red wine vinegar

1 small red onion, finely diced

Preparation time 30 minutes

Makes 8 small salads or 16 large appetizers

BUY AND ARRANGE

Pan-fried chorizo (see p149)
• roasted new potatoes with paprika (see p173) • marinated anchovies (see p30)

PARTNER WITH

Yellow lentil soup (see p44)
• romesco dip (see p56) •
serrano-wrapped shrimp
(see p108)

Spinach and peppered pear salad
with raspberry walnut oil dressing

Walnut oil can make even the most humble lettuce taste impressive. Buy it in small quantities, since it loses its nutty perfume after a short time.

1 Preheat the oven to 400°F (200°C). Spread out the bread cubes on a nonstick baking sheet. Drizzle with the oil, and season with salt and pepper to taste. Bake for 6 minutes, until golden. Remove the croutons from the oven and leave to cool.

2 Roughly chop the pears into ½ in (1-cm) wide slices. Transfer to a small bowl with the freshly ground pepper and 1 tablespoon of the lemon juice, then toss to coat. In another bowl, mix together the onion and remaining juice.

3 Pour the dressing ingredients into a jar, close the lid, and shake well to combine. Arrange the spinach, pears, pecans, Parmesan chips, and croutons in small individual bowls. Just before serving, pour on the dressing.

Prepare ahead
The Parmesan chips, toasted nuts, croutons, and dressing can all be made the day before, and stored in separate airtight containers. The onion can be chopped and marinated in the lemon juice on the morning of serving day.

INGREDIENTS

1-in (2.5-cm) cubes sourdough or French bread, about 2 large handfuls

3 tbsp olive oil

Salt

2 ripe comice or similar pears, quartered and cored

1 tbsp freshly ground pink and black peppercorns, plus more as needed

Juice of 2 lemons

1 small red onion, finely diced

8 large handfuls baby spinach or mesclun (mixed baby lettuces)

1 cup pecans, toasted

1 recipe Parmesan chips (see p31) or ½ cup roughly grated Parmesan

Dressing

2 tbsp balsamic vinegar

1 tbsp raspberry vinegar

1 tbsp Dijon mustard

½ garlic clove, finely chopped

1 shallot, finely chopped

5 tbsp walnut or hazelnut oil

½ tsp each salt and pepper

Preparation time 20 minutes
Cooking time 6 minutes
Makes 8–10 individual cups or 4–6 appetizers

BUY AND ARRANGE	PARTNER WITH
Grilled asparagus with balsamic vinegar (see p172) • crushed feta dip (see p70) • prosciutto-wrapped melon (see p31)	Mozzarella en corroza (see p22) • shrimp and roasted tomatoes (see p145) • chocolate crinkle cookies (see p204)

Three-tomato salad
with goat cheese and croutons

The types of tomatoes listed here are just a guide. Choose a selection of beautiful, ripe varieties. Using both red and yellow tomatoes adds color and interest.

1 Preheat the oven to 400°F (200°C). On a baking sheet, toss the bread cubes with the oil, salt, and pepper. Bake for 6 minutes or until light and golden. Avoid overcooking: you want chewy, not rock-hard, centers. Remove from the oven and leave to cool. Meanwhile, toss the shallots with the lemon juice in a bowl.

2 Place all of the dressing ingredients in a jar, close the lid, and shake well to combine. In a large bowl, combine the tomatoes and basil. Pour the dressing over the salad and turn to coat. Divide the salad between 6–8 small bowls, sprinkle with the goat cheese, and serve.

Prepare ahead

The croutons can be made 2 days in advance and stored in an airtight container. The dressing can be prepared the day before. The tomatoes can be cut 2 hours in advance, but drain off any excess juice before mixing the salad.

INGREDIENTS

4 medium-size slices sourdough, French, or ciabatta bread, cut into ½-in (1-cm) cubes

2 tbsp extra-virgin olive oil

½ tsp each salt and pepper

2 large shallots, finely diced

Juice of ½ lemon

1 lb (500 g) ripe cherry, sugarplum, plum, or grape tomatoes, halved

2 red or yellow tomatoes, quartered

2 yellow and/or red beefsteak tomatoes, cut into bite-sized chunks

Large bunch basil leaves, roughly chopped

4 oz (100 g) firm, mild goat cheese such as chèvre blanc, crumbled

Dressing

½ garlic clove, chopped

1½ tbsp red wine vinegar such as cabernet sauvignon

3½ tbsp extra-virgin olive oil

½ tsp Dijon mustard

Pinch each of salt, pepper, and sugar

Preparation time 10 minutes
Cooking time 6 minutes
Makes 6–8 small salads

BUY AND ARRANGE	PARTNER WITH
Carrots in vinaigrette (see p173) • prosciutto-wrapped melon (see p31) • fresh crab crostini (see p148)	Sicilian artichoke bottoms (see p154) • bresaola and pear rolls (see p188) • chocolate Frangelico pudding (see p200)

Arabian salad
with dill and crispy pita

This lively and colorful salad is a superb addition to any Middle Eastern or Moorish-inspired menu. The punchy flavors can liven up an otherwise plain meat or fish dish.

1 Preheat the oven to 400°F (200°C). Place the diced pita bread on a nonstick baking sheet, spoon on the olive oil, and turn to coat. Bake for about 5 minutes, turning once, until golden and crisp. Remove and leave to cool.

2 To make the dressing, put all the ingredients in a small glass jar, close the lid, and shake well until thoroughly mixed.

3 In a large bowl, combine the lettuce, tomatoes, cucumber, scallions, red pepper, radishes, herbs, and pitas.

4 Pour the dressing over the salad, season to taste with salt and pepper, and toss well. Divide between 8 small bowls or 4 appetizer plates. Sprinkle with pomegranate seeds, if using.

Prepare ahead
The pita chips can be baked and stored in an airtight container for 4 days. The dressing can be made the night before. The salad ingredients can be prepared about 4 hours in advance and kept covered in the refrigerator until ready to combine.

INGREDIENTS

6 pita breads, cut into tiny pieces with scissors

3 tbsp extra-virgin olive oil

1 small head romaine or 2 baby gem lettuce, cut into small pieces

8 oz (225 g) cherry tomatoes, halved

1 medium-sized cucumber, deseeded, or 3 Lebanese mini-cucumbers, finely diced

4 scallions, thinly sliced

1 red pepper, finely diced

6 radishes, thinly sliced

Small bunch fresh dill, chopped

Small bunch fresh mint, finely chopped

Salt and freshly ground black pepper

Pomegranate seeds, to garnish

Dressing
1 small garlic clove, crushed

½ tsp each salt and pepper

1 tsp lemon juice

2 tsp red wine vinegar or pomegranate molasses

⅓ cup extra-virgin olive oil

Preparation time 20 minutes

Makes 8 small bowls or 4 starters

BUY AND ARRANGE	PARTNER WITH
Hummus with smoked paprika (*see p70*) • pan-fried chorizo (*see p149*) • Middle Eastern pastries (*see p214*)	Spinach and yogurt dip (*see p66*) • saffron feta phyllo triangles (*see p182*) • cumin lamb skewers (*see p112*)

Seared duck and mango salad
with green papaya

Green papaya can be found in Thai supermarkets. To preserve its crunch, slice into julienne strips instead of grating. If you can't find green papaya, replace it with rice noodles.

1 Preheat the oven to 400°F (200°C). Using a sharp knife, cut a crosshatch pattern into the duck skin. Combine the marinade ingredients and place in a bowl. Add the duck breasts, coat, and leave to marinate for at least 15 minutes.

2 Heat a nonstick pan over high heat until very hot. Meanwhile, remove the duck from the marinade, wipe, place skin-side down in the pan, and brown. Reduce the heat to low and continue to cook until the fat is melted and the skin is thin and crispy. Place the duck on a nonstick baking sheet and bake in the oven for 10 minutes. Remove and allow to rest for 10 minutes before slicing thinly.

3 Divide the papaya, mango, and herbs among 8 small bowls. Top with the duck, garnish with scallions, and pour on the lime and chili pepper dressing. Sprinkle with the peanuts and serve.

Prepare ahead
The duck can be left to marinate overnight in the refrigerator. The salad ingredients and dressing can be assembled in the morning of serving day, and tossed just before serving. The salad can be dressed 1 hour before serving.

INGREDIENTS

2 boneless duck breasts

1 medium green papaya, sliced into julienne strips

1 very firm mango, sliced into julienne strips

Small handful Thai or Mediterranean basil leaves

Small handful mint leaves

Small handful cilantro leaves

4 scallions, sliced lengthwise

1 recipe lime and chili pepper dressing (see p216), to serve

3 tbsp crushed roasted peanuts, to garnish

Marinade

2 tbsp soy sauce

1 tbsp honey

1 tbsp grated fresh ginger root

1 tsp cracked black pepper

Preparation and cooking time
35 minutes, plus 15 minutes marinating time

Makes 8 small salads or 4 appetizers

BUY AND ARRANGE	PARTNER WITH
Fresh oysters (see p148) • selection of sushi (see p31) • freshly sliced pineapple (see p215)	Pork and shrimp dumplings (see p184) • crispy scallops (see p24) • miso monkfish bites (see p140)

Quick salads
buy-and-arrange ideas to create simple salads

With just a few raw ingredients, some washing, a little chopping, and a quickly mixed dressing, you can create a range of enticing, fresh salads. Try any of the ideas below as a quick alternative to the other salad dishes featured in this chapter. These short recipes are just a guide, so experiment with different leaves and dressings.

Shaved celery salad with mushroom and pecorino

Slice enough white mushrooms and celery hearts to make 2 handfuls each. Mix in a bowl with 1 handful grated pecorino cheese. In a separate bowl, mix 1 tablespoon red wine vinegar with 2 tablespoons extra-virgin olive oil, then season. Serve the salad drizzled with dressing.

Fig, prosciutto, and mozzarella salad

Cut 4 ripe figs and 4 slices prosciutto into quarters and arrange them on a platter with a small bunch of basil leaves. Rip 2 mozzarella balls into small pieces and add them to the plate. Scatter over the platter 1 tablespoon balsamic vinegar with 2 tablespoons extra-virgin olive oil, then season with salt and pepper. Serve the salad on the platter or in separate small bowls.

Baby lettuce with walnut oil and sherry vinegar

Place 5 generous handfuls of fresh mixed baby lettuces in a mixing bowl. In a separate bowl, mix 1 tablespoon sherry vinegar with 2 tablespoons walnut oil, then season with salt and pepper. Toss the salad with the dressing, then divide between small serving bowls.

Palm heart and avocado salad

Drain a 14-oz (400-g) can of palm hearts. Slice the palm hearts and 2 avocados into chunky pieces and place them in a bowl. Add a small handful of thickly grated parmesan and combine well. In a separate bowl, mix 1 tablespoon red wine vinegar with 2 tablespoons extra-virgin olive oil, then season with salt and pepper. Serve the salad in small bowls, drizzled with the dressing.

Radicchio, orange, and arugula salad

Mix together 2 large handfuls each of arugula and chopped radicchio leaves in a bowl. Cut the segments from 2 oranges and add to the salad. In a separate bowl, mix 1 tablespoon balsamic vinegar with 2 tablespoons extra-virgin olive oil and season with salt and pepper. Toss the salad with the dressing and serve in small bowls.

Tomato and coconut sambal

In a bowl, mix together 2 large handfuls chopped cherry tomatoes; 1 medium cucumber, diced; 1 small red onion, diced; 1 small handful chopped cilantro; 2 tablespoons shredded coconut, ½ teaspoon cumin seeds; ½ teaspoon chili powder, and the juice of half a lemon. Serve in small bowls.

Watermelon and feta salad

Cut a small watermelon into cubes or slices and arrange on a platter, or on smaller serving plates. Add 1 small handful mint leaves, a chunk of feta cheese, crumbled, and 1 thinly sliced red onion. In a separate bowl, mix the juice of 1 lemon, 1 tablespoon balsamic vinegar, and 1 tablespoon extra-virgin olive oil. Drizzle over the salad.

Frisee with quail's eggs

Mix 1 tablespoon red wine vinegar with 2 tablespoons extra-virgin olive oil, then season with salt and pepper. Mix the dressing with 5 handfuls frisee lettuce (or curly endive) and transfer to small bowls. Top with 6 halved soft-boiled quail's eggs.

Chicory salad with anchovy lemon dressing

Using a mortar and pestle, pound together 1 anchovy and 1 clove garlic. Mix in the juice of 1 lemon and 2 tablespoons extra-virgin olive oil. Combine with 4 heads chicory and season with salt and pepper. Serve in small bowls.

Watercress salad with scallions

Toss together 5 large handfuls watercress or other spicy lettuce with 2 sliced scallions. In a separate bowl, mix together 1 tablespoon sesame seeds, 1 teaspoon soy sauce, 1 teaspoon balsamic vinegar, and1 tablespoon olive oil, then season with salt and pepper. Toss the salad with the dressing and serve in small bowls.

Watermelon and feta salad

Asian cucumber salad

Thinly slice 4 tiny cucumbers or cut 1 large cucumber into ¾-in (2-cm) cubes. In a small bowl, mix together 1 tablespoon rice wine vinegar with 1 teaspoon sugar, then season with salt and pepper. Mix the cucumber cubes or slices with the dressing, then serve in small bowls.

Lebanese salad plate

Arrange the leaves of 1 small romaine heart, some halved Lebanese cucumbers or very small cucumbers, a handful of whole radishes, sprigs of fresh parsley and tarragon, and 1 thickly sliced red pepper on a serving plate.

What is it about food on a stick that makes it so enticing? Perhaps it's the ease of sliding off each bite as you eat, savoring the taste, then casually discarding the skewer. Choose your skewers with flair; metal or bamboo ones are fine, but lemongrass stalks or sugar cane are more interesting.

Skewers

Citrus swordfish brochettes
with pomegranate dipping sauce

Swordfish is a meaty, firm type of fish, which makes it particularly well-suited for threading onto skewers. The sharp citrus flavors complement its subtle taste.

1   Rub the fish with the olive oil and garlic, then sprinkle with the lemon and orange zest, chili peppers, fennel seed, salt, and pepper. Leave to marinate in the refrigerator for 30 minutes to 2 hours.

2   Thread two pieces of fish onto each skewer. Heat a nonstick frying pan over medium-high heat and dry-fry until browned on all sides. This cooking method creates the best color, but you could also cook the skewers under the broiler or on a barbecue grill. Serve with the pomegranate dipping sauce and lemon or lime wedges.

Prepare ahead

The dipping sauce, fish cubes, and marinade ingredients may be prepared the day before and refrigerated. You can pan-fry the fish 2 hours before serving, but leave it underdone and gently reheat in an oven preheated to 400°F (200°C).

INGREDIENTS

1 lb (450 g) swordfish, cut into fifty 1-in (2.5-cm) cubes

1 tbsp extra-virgin olive oil

1 garlic clove, crushed

Grated zest of 1 lemon

Grated zest of 1 orange

½ tsp crushed dried chili peppers

1½ tbsp fennel seed, crushed with a mortar and pestle

½ tsp each salt and pepper

25 metal or wooden skewers (if wooden, soak in water for 1 hour to prevent burning)

1 recipe pomegranate dipping sauce (see p217), to serve

Lemon or lime wedges, to serve

Preparation and cooking time
20 minutes

Makes 25 skewers

BUY AND ARRANGE

Hummus with smoked paprika (see p70) • watermelon and feta salad (see p93) • Middle Eastern pastries (see p214)

PARTNER WITH

Yellow lentil soup (see p44) • garbanzo and chili pepper dip (see p68) • pan-fried halloumi salad (see p82)

Saffron chicken skewers
with sweet tomato jam

This marinade is based on the Spanish tapas dish pinchitos murunos, consisting of pork fillet grilled with saffron and spices. Pimenton (sweet, smoked Spanish paprika) may be found in good delicatessens or large supermarkets.

1 Combine all of the marinade ingredients in a bowl, mixing thoroughly. Flatten the cubes of chicken slightly, add to the marinade, and turn to coat on all sides. Leave to marinate in the refrigerator for at least 1–2 hours.

2 Preheat the oven to 400°F (200°C). Thread one piece of chicken onto each skewer and season. Heat the oil in a nonstick frying pan, add the skewers, and fry to color each side. Transfer to a nonstick baking sheet, cover with foil, and place in the oven for 5 minutes. Alternatively, cook the skewers under the broiler or on a barbecue grill.

3 Arrange the chicken skewers on a serving plate, with the sweet tomato jam and the cilantro.

Prepare ahead
The jam can be prepared up to 4 days in advance. The skewers may be marinated 1 day ahead and pan-fried up to 2 hours before cooking in the oven.

INGREDIENTS

3 chicken breasts or boneless skinless thighs, cut into 25 1-in (2.5-cm) cubes

25 wooden skewers, soaked in water for 1 hour, to prevent burning

Salt and pepper

1–2 tbsp olive oil

1 recipe sweet tomato jam (see p218), to serve

A few sprigs cilantro, to garnish

Marinade

½ tsp each coriander seeds, cumin seeds, and fennel seeds, roughly ground

1 tsp pimenton

2 garlic cloves, crushed

Pinch saffron, infused in 1 tbsp boiling water

1 tbsp red wine vinegar

1 tbsp olive oil

Preparation time 10 minutes
Cooking time 15 minutes
Makes 25 skewers

BUY AND ARRANGE	PARTNER WITH
Roasted new potatoes with paprika (see p173) • crushed feta dip (see p70) • spice-dusted shrimp (see p148)	Pan-fried halloumi salad (see p82) • smoky eggplant puree (see p64) • Arabian salad (see p88)

Colors

- Creamy ivory
- Warm tangerine
- Rose pink
- Gold or silver
- Cool violet

Tableware

- Tea lights and candles
- Gold-rimmed glasses
- Creamy-colored linens
- Red rose petals
- Embroidered napkins

Middle Eastern delights

Pack your bags for the spice trail. Begin your journey in Iran, continue on through Turkey, stay a little while in Morocco, and linger in Spain. These countries' cuisines have each been molded by a legacy of Persian cooking brilliance.

A traditional Middle Eastern meal is composed of a variety of smaller dishes, which is the classic style of mezze and tapas. These diminutive little bites, from garbanzo dips to savory pastries, offer your taste buds truly memorable eating experiences. Lemons, olives, coriander, saffron, rose water, dried apricots, and pistachios are the stars of this exemplary food. Aromatic spices, fresh herbs, flaky pastry, and creamy legumes are present in endless, delicious variations.

So, light every candle you own and fill your home with a sensual glow. For the table, seek out creamy-colored linens and lightweight fabrics, such as voile; gold-rimmed glassware and tea glasses; and scatter red rose petals over everything. Picture Arabian nights and recreate the soft, romantic atmosphere that makes the Middle East so special.

Flavors

- Pungent cumin
- Sharp lemon
- Luxurious saffron
- Dried fruits
- Fragrant rose water

Nibbles

- Pistachios (*see p31*)
- Marinated black olives (*see p30*)
- Hummus with smoked paprika (*see p70*)
- Sumac-dusted shrimp (*see p148*)
- Crushed feta dip (*see p70*)

Menu

Garbanzo and chili pepper dip
with pita crisps

Saffron chicken skewers
with sweet tomato jam

Saffron feta phyllo triangles
with preserved lemon and onion

Pan-fried halloumi salad
with black olive dressing

Yellow lentil soup with prunes,
pomegranates, and apricots

Cardamom-poached apricots
with mascarpone and pistachios

BUY AND ARRANGE
Marinated black olives (*see p30*)

Oranges with rose water and
pomegranate seeds (*see p214*)

Crushed feta dip (*see p70*)

Garbanzo and chili pepper
dip (*see p68*)

Saffron chicken skewers
(*see p98*)

Saffron feta phyllo
triangles (*see p182*)

Pan-fried halloumi salad
(*see p82*)

Yellow lentil soup
(*see p44*)

Cardamom-poached
apricots (*see p211*)

Two days before
- Make sweet tomato jam
- Make yellow lentil soup
- Marinate black olives

The night before
- Make pita crisps for the
  garbanzo dip
- Marinate saffron chicken
- Assemble saffron feta phyllo
  triangles
- Make cardamom-poached
  apricots

In the morning
- Puree base of garbanzo dip
- Cut oranges and make black-
  olive dressing for halloumi salad
- Make oranges with rose water

Orange champagne cocktails

Oranges are a quintessential fruit of the Middle East, and they act as the perfect partner to champagne.

INGREDIENTS

6 measures orange vodka

6 sugar cubes

6 raspberries

6 dashes Angostura bitters

1 bottle champagne or sparkling white wine

Zest of 1 orange

Makes 6 cocktails

Add 1 measure of vodka, 1 sugar cube, 1 raspberry, and 1 dash of Angostura bitters to each champagne glass. Pour the champagne in. Use pomegranate seeds or cubes of orange in place of the raspberries, if you wish. Serve topped with small slivers of orange zest.

One to two hours before
- Finish garbanzo dip
- Sear saffron chicken
- Pan-fry halloumi for the salad
- Plate cardamom-poached apricots
- Reheat yellow lentil soup
- Organize cocktail ingredients

Half an hour before
- Reheat sweet tomato jam
- Cook saffron chicken skewers
- Plate oranges with rose water
- Bake saffron feta phyllo triangles

Half an hour before
- Plate garbanzo dip with pita crisps
- Plate saffron chicken skewers
- Plate halloumi salad with black olive dressing
- Plate saffron feta phyllo triangles
- Pour yellow lentil soup
- Pour champagne cocktails

Lemongrass beef skewers
with sticky cucumber and peanut sauce

If you are short on time, serve these skewers with a bottled sweet chili-pepper dipping sauce. Sirloin or rump steak, cut into very thin strips, can be used in place of the beef fillet.

1 If using beef fillet, cut into 1½-in (4-cm) cubes. If using sirloin or rump steak, cut into very thin strips. Cut away the top two thirds of the lemongrass stalks, remove the outer leaves, and chop the hearts finely.

2 Combine the lemongrass, garlic, fish sauce, sesame oil, five-spice powder, honey, and cilantro in a shallow bowl. Add the beef, turn to coat, and marinate for at least 10 minutes. Remove the meat from the marinade and thread the beef onto the skewers.

3 Heat the vegetable oil over medium-high heat in a nonstick frying pan. Add the skewers and brown on all sides: they will need only a few minutes since the meat is very tender. Remove from the heat, cover with foil, and leave to rest for 5 minutes. Alternatively, cook under the broiler or on a barbecue grill. Serve the skewers on lettuce leaves, accompanied by the sticky cucumber and peanut sauce.

Prepare ahead

The meat can be marinated up to 2 days ahead and the sauce can be made on the morning of serving day. Grill and par-cook the skewers a few hours ahead, refrigerate, then complete cooking just before serving.

INGREDIENTS

1 lb (450 g) beef tenderloin, sirloin, or rump steak

4 lemongrass stalks

2 garlic cloves, finely chopped

2 tbsp fish sauce

2 tbsp sesame oil

1½ tsp five-spice powder

2 tbsp honey

Small bunch cilantro, chopped

25 metal or wooden skewers (if wooden, soak for 30 minutes to prevent burning)

1 tbsp vegetable oil

Lettuce leaves, to serve

1 recipe sticky cucumber and peanut sauce (see p218), to serve

Preparation and cooking time 30 minutes

Makes 20–25 skewers

BUY AND ARRANGE

Asian cucumber salad (see p93) • spicy peanut dip (see p71) • exotic fruit salad (see p215)

PARTNER WITH

Seared sesame tuna (see p138) • pork satay (see p109) • avocado crostini (see p164)

Halloumi and sourdough spiedini
with lemon anchovy drizzle

Mozzarella is great in place of the halloumi here, but it melts quickly, so keep a careful eye on it. Use a different bread, if you prefer, but remember to have a little crust on each cube so that they all stay on the skewer.

1 Cut the halloumi (or mozzarella) into 32 1-in (2½-cm) cubes. Slice the bread into 32 1-in (2½-cm) cubes, retaining the crusts for strength.

2 To make the drizzle, crush the garlic and anchovies to a paste with a mortar and pestle. Transfer to a saucepan. Add the butter and olive oil and simmer over low heat for 5 minutes. Remove from the heat and stir in the lemon zest, lemon juice, and parsley.

3 Thread the cheese and bread onto the skewers, alternating 2 cubes of bread and 2 pieces of cheese. Brush with the drizzle and season to taste with salt and pepper. Pan-fry in a nonstick frying pan over medium heat until golden on all sides. Alternatively, cook under the broiler or on a barbecue grill.

Prepare ahead

The recipe can be made on the morning of serving day, stored in the refrigerator, then brushed with the drizzle just before cooking.

INGREDIENTS

28 oz (800 g) halloumi

Small loaf of sourdough bread

16 6-in (15-cm) wooden skewers, presoaked to prevent burning

Drizzle

1 garlic clove, finely chopped

2 anchovies, rinsed and finely chopped

2 tbsp unsalted butter

4 tbsp extra-virgin olive oil

1 tsp lemon zest

Juice of 1½ lemons

Small handful fresh parsley leaves, finely chopped

Salt and pepper

Preparation time 20 minutes
Cooking time 15 minutes
Makes 16 skewers

BUY AND ARRANGE

Shaved celery salad (*see p92*) • avocado with balsamic vinegar (*see p173*) • radishes with tapenade (*see p173*)

PARTNER WITH

Meatball and pecorino soup (*see p48*) • roasted shrimp and tomatoes (*see p145*) • chocolate Frangelico pudding (*see p200*)

Serrano-wrapped shrimp
with roasted pepper salsa

Piquillo peppers are smoked, roasted Spanish peppers that are sold in jars and can be located in supermarkets. If you can't find them, use two large roasted red peppers instead.

1   Wrap each shrimp in a strip of ham, then thread onto a skewer.

2   To make the salsa, heat 4 tablespoons of the oil in a saucepan. Add the garlic slices and sauté over low heat for 3–5 minutes, until golden brown. Remove the garlic and set aside.

3   Add the vinegar, honey, salt, and pepper to the oil in the pan, and whisk over low heat, until combined. Transfer to a small bowl, and stir in the garlic, onion, peppers, and parsley.

4   To make the skewers, heat the oil in a frying pan until hot, and fry the skewers for about 1 minute on all sides, until the ham is golden and the shrimp are cooked through. Arrange the salsa in small bowls and top each with 1–2 skewers.

Prepare ahead
The skewers and salsa can be assembled the day before and refrigerated. Bring the salsa to room temperature before serving.

INGREDIENTS

24 large shrimp, peeled and deveined

8 slices serrano ham or prosciutto, cut into 3 strips

24 wooden skewers, soaked in water for 30 minutes

1 tbsp extra-virgin olive oil

Salsa

4 tbsp extra-virgin olive oil

2 garlic cloves, thinly sliced

2 tbsp sherry vinegar

2 tsp honey

½ tsp each salt and pepper

1 small red onion, finely diced

8 roasted piquillo peppers, finely diced

4 tbsp finely chopped, fresh flat-leaf parsley

Preparation time 30 minutes
Cooking time 10 minutes
Makes 24 skewers

BUY AND ARRANGE

Palm heart and avocado salad (see p92) • crushed feta dip (see p70) • ice cream with sweet sherry (see p214)

PARTNER WITH

Crispy chorizo quesadillas (see p186) • beef and sweet potato skewers (see p114) • beet pesto (see p67)

Pork satay on lemongrass
with spicy peanut sauce

The lemongrass skewers add fragrance and interest, but substitute them with presoaked wooden skewers, if you wish.

1 Preheat the oven to 400°F (200°C). Trim the tops of 4 lemongrass stalks, remove the leaves, and finely chop the hearts. In a bowl, mix the cilantro, chopped lemongrass, pork, garlic, shallots, fish sauce, egg, curry paste, and pepper. Shape into 20 balls.

2 Slice the remaining lemongrass lengthwise to make 20 sticks. Thread the meatballs onto the skewers, molding them on. Sprinkle with the flour and set aside.

3 Heat the oil in a frying pan and fry the skewers for 1 minute on each side, until golden. Place on a nonstick baking tray, cover with foil, and bake in the oven for 5 minutes. Serve with the spicy peanut sauce and garnish with cilantro.

Prepare ahead

Prepare the sauce and meatballs a day ahead and refrigerate. The meat can be put on skewers early on the same day you plan to serve them.

INGREDIENTS

16 lemongrass stalks

Small bunch fresh cilantro leaves, chopped, a few sprigs saved to garnish

1 lb (450 g) lean ground pork

3 garlic cloves, finely chopped

3 shallots, finely chopped

2 tbsp fish sauce

1 egg, beaten

1 tbsp red curry paste

½ tsp pepper

2 tbsp rice flour or all-purpose flour, for dusting

1 tbsp vegetable oil

1 recipe spicy peanut sauce (see p218), to serve

Preparation time 20 minutes
Cooking time 30 minutes
Makes 20 skewers

BUY AND ARRANGE

Caramelized grilled pineapple (see p214) • shrimp and cucumber skewers (see p149) • steamed edamame (see p173)

PARTNER WITH

Thai corn fritters (see p26) • red curry pumpkin soup (see p46) • seared duck and mango salad (see p90)

Salmon pineapple skewers
with pepper glaze and lime crème fraîche

Dried chili peppers impart a depth to glazes and sauces that fresh ones can't match. Anchos have a subtle, fruity scent. If you can't find them, use any other large dried variety.

1 To make the glaze, place the dried pepper in a bowl of boiling water and soak for 15 minutes. Meanwhile, in a large, dry, nonstick frying pan, pan-fry the garlic and onion over medium-low heat, stirring, for about 7 minutes, until blackened on all sides. Remove from the heat and allow to cool, then peel the garlic.

2 Drain the chili pepper and place it in a blender or food processor with the garlic, onion, vinegar, sugar, and salt. Puree until smooth, then pour into a small bowl. In a separate bowl, mix the lime zest and juice with the crème fraîche, and set aside.

3 Preheat the oven to 400°F (200°C). Thread one salmon and one pineapple cube onto each skewer. Brush with the glaze. Heat the oil over medium-high heat in a nonstick frying pan and cook the skewers in batches, searing for 1 minute to color each side. Place on a baking sheet, cover with foil, and heat through in the oven for 5 minutes. Alternatively, the skewers can be broiled or grilled. Serve with cilantro sprigs and the lime crème fraîche.

Prepare ahead

The glaze can be made 1 week in advance and refrigerated. The skewers can be assembled the day before and refrigerated.

INGREDIENTS

1 cup crème fraîche or sour cream

Grated zest and juice of 1 lime

1 lb (450 g) thick salmon filet, sliced into 1-in (2.5-cm) cubes

1 small pineapple, cut into 1-in (2.5-cm) cubes

20 metal or wooden skewers (if wooden, soak in water for 30 minutes to prevent burning)

2 tbsp vegetable oil

Chopped fresh cilantro, to garnish

Glaze

1 dried ancho pepper, deseeded and stem removed

6 garlic cloves, unpeeled

1 small yellow onion, thickly sliced

¼ cup cider vinegar

4 tbsp soft light brown sugar

½ tsp salt

Preparation time 40 minutes
Cooking time 20 minutes
Makes 20–25 skewers

BUY AND ARRANGE	PARTNER WITH
Sweet potato wedges with cumin (see p172) • fruit salsa (see p70) • mango fool (see p215)	Smoky black bean dip (see p58) • grilled butterfly shrimp (see p141) • crab and Gruyére nachos (see p142)

Cumin lamb skewers
with red onion parsley salad

Use the soft flatbread to scoop up luscious mouthfuls of the salad and lamb. If you can't find the molasses, use a tablespoon each of honey and lemon juice in its place.

1 Combine the marinade ingredients in a medium-sized bowl. Add the lamb, toss to coat, and leave to marinate for at least 30 minutes. Thread one or two lamb cubes onto each skewer, then set aside until ready to cook.

2 For the salad, place the onions in a bowl with the lemon juice, salt, and pepper. Turn to coat, and leave for 5 minutes to reduce the raw taste of the onion. Add the parsley, paprika, and oil. Mix well and set aside.

3 Heat the vegetable oil in a nonstick frying pan over medium-high heat. Add the skewers and brown the meat well on all sides. Remove and place under foil for 5 minutes, to rest. Alternatively, broil the skewers or cook on a barbecue grill. Serve on small plates or on a platter with the salad and flatbread. Garnish with pomegranate seeds, if desired.

Prepare ahead

The lamb can be left to marinate up to 2 days in advance. It may then be browned 4 hours before serving, refrigerated, and finished off for 5 minutes in an oven heated to 400°F (200°C). The salad may be assembled 2 hours in advance.

INGREDIENTS

1 lb (450 g) lamb filet or leg steaks, cut into 1½-in (4-cm) cubes

20–25 skewers (if wooden, soak for 30 minutes to prevent burning)

1 tbsp vegetable oil

Pita or other flatbread, to serve

Fresh pomegranate seeds, to garnish (*optional*)

Marinade

4 tbsp pomegranate molasses

1 tsp cumin seeds, lightly toasted

4 garlic cloves, crushed

1 tsp salt

1 tsp crushed black pepper

Salad

1 medium-sized red onion, cut into thin half-moons

Juice of ½ lemon

½ tsp salt

½ tsp pepper

Large handful parsley leaves, roughly chopped

½ tsp paprika

1 tbsp extra-virgin olive oil

Preparation and cooking time
20 minutes, plus marinating time (30 minutes or up to 2 days)

Makes 20–25 skewers

BUY AND ARRANGE	PARTNER WITH
Roasted new potatoes with paprika (*see p173*) • yogurt and dill dip (*see p71*) • black olives with orange (*see p30*)	Spinach and yogurt dip (*see p66*) • saffron feta phyllo triangles (*see p182*) • Arabian salad (*see p88*)

Beef and sweet potato skewers
with chimichurri sauce

Chimichurri is a punchy chili pepper and herb sauce from South America, and it pairs well with meat. Other tender cuts of beef can work nearly as well as filets.

1 Combine the marinade ingredients in a bowl, stirring well to mix. Add the meat, turn to coat, and leave to marinate for an hour.

2 Meanwhile, preheat the oven to 400°F (200°C). Place the sweet potato pieces in a roasting pan with the oil, turn to coat, season with salt and pepper, and roast for 20 minutes. Remove from the oven and leave to cool.

3 To make the sauce, place all of the ingredients in a bowl and mix well. The chopping and mixing can be done in a food processor, adding the peppers and garlic first, for a smoother consistency.

4 Thread the skewers with the meat and sweet potato. Set aside. Heat the broiler to high and broil the skewers for about 2 minutes on each side, until crispy on the edges. Cover with foil and allow to rest for 5 minutes before serving warm, with the sauce. Alternatively, they can be cooked on a barbecue grill.

Prepare ahead

The beef can be marinated for up to 2 days, covered in the refrigerator, and skewered the day before serving. The sauce can be made 4 hours in advance.

INGREDIENTS

1 lb (450 g) beef filet or sirloin steak, cut into 1½-in (4-cm) cubes

3 sweet potatoes, cut into 1½-in (4-cm) chunks

2 tbsp olive oil

Salt and pepper, to taste

20 metal or wooden skewers (if wooden, soak in water for 30 minutes to prevent burning)

Marinade

1 tbsp olive oil

1 tbsp ground cumin

½ tsp each salt and pepper

Sauce

1 jalapeño or other green chili pepper, deseeded and finely chopped

2 garlic cloves, finely chopped

Small bunch fresh cilantro, finely chopped

Large bunch flat-leaf parsley, finely chopped

½ tsp pimenton

½ cup extra-virgin olive oil

3 tbsp red wine vinegar, such as cabernet sauvignon or strong chianti

½ tsp each salt and pepper

Preparation time 20 minutes, plus 1 hour marinating time

Cooking time 25 minutes

Makes 20 skewers

BUY AND ARRANGE	PARTNER WITH
Palm heart and avocado salad (see p92) • Spanish deli plate (see p30) • pan-fried chorizo (see p149)	Smoky black bean dip (see p58) • crab and Gruyère nachos (see p142) • grilled butterfly shrimp (see p141)

Whether you prefer to use the bones of cutlets as natural brochettes, or decide to choose a faithful fork, eating meat is a tactile experience with a primitive allure. Select some fresh herbs and spices or prepare the marinade, and you're ready for some serious sustenance.

Meat

Rosemary lamb chops
with fresh mint and parsley sauce

This simple but exquisite dish works best using two racks of lamb. Buy them cleaned of fat so the chops can be picked up and eaten by hand. Alternatively, use 12 lamb cutlets.

1   Combine the oil, vinegar, and rosemary in a large bowl. Cover the meat with a sheet of waxed paper or baking parchment and flatten slightly with a rolling pin or meat mallet. Add the meat to the oil mixture, turn to coat, and marinate for at least 1 hour.

2   Preheat the broiler to high. Remove the chops from the marinade, and cook under the broiler for 2 minutes on each side. Cover with foil and leave to rest for a few minutes before serving with the fresh mint and parsley sauce.

Prepare ahead
The chops can be marinated, covered, and refrigerated up to 2 days in advance. The sauce may be made earlier on the same day you plan to serve the chops.

INGREDIENTS

1 tbsp olive oil

2 tbsp balsamic vinegar

1 tbsp fresh chopped rosemary, stems removed

2 racks of lamb, cut into chops and bones cleaned of fat

1 recipe fresh mint and parsley sauce (see p216), to serve

Preparation time 15 minutes, plus 1 hour marinating time

Cooking time 8 minutes

Makes 12 cutlets

BUY AND ARRANGE

Frisee with quail's eggs (see p93) • roasted shallots (see p173) • biscotti, mascarpone, and dessert wine (see p215)

PARTNER WITH

Fried artichokes, Roman style (see p12) • orange and beet soup (see p40) • farro salad (see p78)

Crispy pork larb and mango
in lettuce cups with pepper-lime dressing

"Larb" is the Thai word for ground meat. In this recipe, it is pan-fried until crispy, then tossed with dressing. Try to use a mango that is ripe, yet firm enough to make it easy to chop.

1 Cut away the base and top third of the lemongrass, and finely slice the soft, inner part. Add the oil to a large, heavy-bottomed sauté pan or wok, and heat to medium-high. Add the lemongrass and fry for about 2 minutes, stirring, until soft.

2 Raise the heat to high, add the pork, and cook until crispy and brown underneath before breaking it up with a fork. Stir in the sugar and continue to fry, stirring, for about 5 minutes, until thoroughly cooked through. Remove from the heat and set aside.

3 Pour the dressing over the pork, add the onion, mango, and cilantro, then stir gently to combine. Use the baby lettuce leaves as serving bowls or to scoop up the meat.

Prepare ahead
You can prepare the ingredients and the dressing a few hours before serving the pork. About one hour before serving, and while it is still warm, dress the pork.

INGREDIENTS

3 stalks lemongrass

2 tbsp vegetable oil

1 lb (450 g) lean ground pork

1 tbsp soft brown sugar

1 recipe lime and chili pepper dressing (see p216)

1 small red onion, finely diced

1 ripe but firm mango, diced

3 tbsp fresh chopped cilantro leaves

20 heart of romaine lettuce leaves, chilled, to serve

Preparation time 20 minutes
Cooking time 10 minutes
Makes 20 lettuce cups

BUY AND ARRANGE

Spicy peanut sauce (see p218) • shrimp and cucumber skewers (see p149) • exotic fruit salad (see p215)

PARTNER WITH

Thai corn fritters (see p26) • seared sesame tuna (see p138) • grilled baby eggplants (see p170)

Colors

- Sky blue
- Mustard yellow
- French blue
- Delicate lavender
- Bone white

Tableware

- Distressed white china
- Bone-handled cutlery
- Yellow mimosa flowers
- Rustic terra-cotta plates
- Plain linen napkins

Mediterranean table

In the countries that sit along the Mediterranean Sea, you will encounter people who are perhaps more passionate and spirited about food than those you meet anywhere else. Food is paramount here, and life revolves around mealtimes. Of course, if we could all eat al fresco year-round, under the gently soothing sun, we might quickly adjust our priorities, too.

If you want to be assured of creating outstanding Mediterranean food, then it is important to track the seasons. Each brings its own fresh bounty: spring artichokes, summer tomatoes, fall mushrooms, and bitter winter radicchio. Conveniently, grassy extra-virgin olive oils, capers, anchovies, and nutty Parmesan remain all year. Most herbs are embraced in Mediterranean cuisine; sage, basil, parsley, and dill all make an appearance, adding freshness and perfume.

To dress the table, opt for cheerful sky blue or earthy mustard linen cloths, rustic white or terra-cotta plates and bowls, and pleasantly worn plain steel or bone-handled cutlery. Fill a large water pitcher with fresh flowers, such as yellow mimosa, twist open a Campari soda, and bring the warmth and glow of Mediterranean sunshine into your home.

Flavors

- Grassy olive oil
- Sage, basil, parsley, and dill
- Salty capers and anchovies
- Fragrant cheeses
- Fresh lemon

Nibbles

- Marinated anchovies (*see p30*)
- Parmesan crisps (*see p31*)
- Prosciutto-wrapped melon (*see p31*)
- Roasted garlic with bread (*see p71*)
- Spanish or Italian deli plate (*see p30*)

Menu

Fried artichokes, Roman style
with saffron aioli

Bresaola and pear rolls
with arugula and parmesan

Three tomato salad
with goat cheese and croutons

Gorgonzola crostini
with garlic greens and raisins

Rosemary lamb cutlets
with fresh mint and parsley sauce

Chocolate Frangelico pudding
with hazelnuts

BUY AND ARRANGE

Pesto and aioli with grissini
breadsticks (see p70)

Marinated green olives with celery
(see p30)

Prosciutto-wrapped melon
(see p31)

Fried artichokes, Roman
style (see p12)

Bresaola and pear rolls
(see p188)

Three-tomato salad
(see p86)

Gorgonzola crostini
(see p166)

Rosemary lamb cutlets
(see p118)

Chocolate Frangelico
pudding (see p200)

Two days before
- Make croutons for tomato salad
- Make crostini
- Marinate lamb cutlets
- Marinate green olives

The night before
- Prepare artichokes and leave to
  soak in lemon water
- Make saffron aioli
- Make chocolate Frangelico
  puddings

Four hours before
- Make bresaola and pear rolls
- Chop tomatoes for salad
- Make prosciutto-wrapped
  melon

Blood orange campari soda

Campari has a slightly bitter taste that mixes well with sweet blood-orange juice and bubbly soda water. Italians are fond of it as a cool and refreshing aperitif.

INGREDIENTS

Ice

½ cup Campari

1 pint (½ liter) soda water

1 pint (½ liter) blood-orange juice or tangerine juice

1 orange, sliced, to garnish

Makes 4 cocktails

Half-fill 4 tall highball glasses with ice. Pour the campari over, dividing it between the glasses. Add the blood-orange juice and soda, again dividing them between the glasses. Decorate each glass with a slice of orange.

One hour before
- Remove olives from refrigerator
- Fry artichokes; keep warm in low oven
- Make greens for Gorgonzola crostini
- Organize cocktail ingredients

At the last minute
- Plate artichokes with saffron aioli
- Plate bresaola and pear rolls
- Finish three tomato salad; plate
- Plate lamb cutlets with fresh mint and parsley sauce
- Plate prosciutto-wrapped melon
- Pour cocktails

Half an hour before
- Assemble tomato salad without basil and dressing
- Finish Gorgonzola crostini; plate
- Sear lamb cutlets and keep warm under foil
- Plate pesto, aioli, and grissini breadsticks

Seared cinnamon duck
with mango chutney and poppadom

The duck in this recipe benefits vastly from overnight marinating; the process intensifies its flavor enormously. It's fine to buy your favorite chutney if you don't have time to make it yourself.

1　Cut a crosshatch pattern into the skin of the duck. Place in a shallow bowl with all the marinade ingredients. Turn to coat, and leave to marinate for at least an hour, preferably overnight.

2　Preheat the oven to 400°F (200°C). Remove the duck from the marinade and drain on paper towels. Heat a nonstick frying pan to high, add the duck, fat-side down, and brown. Reduce the heat to low and melt the duck fat for about 5 minutes, until clear and very thin.

3　Place the duck in a small baking dish and roast in the oven for 10 minutes. Remove and leave to rest for 10 minutes on a cutting board, then slice very thinly. To serve, arrange the duck in small bowls with a spoonful of chutney, arugula, and pieces of poppadom or slivers of naan bread.

Prepare ahead

The duck can be marinated for up to 2 days. If it is to be served cold, it can be cooked the day before serving. If it is to be eaten warm, it can be browned the day before. The chutney can be made a week in advance and refrigerated.

INGREDIENTS

2 boneless duck breasts

1 recipe mango chutney (see p216), to serve

2 handfuls arugula, to serve

Indian poppadoms or naan bread, to serve

Marinade

1 tbsp soy sauce

1 tsp honey

½ tsp Chinese five-spice powder

½ tsp ground cinnamon

½-in (1-cm) piece fresh ginger, grated

½ tsp fresh cracked pepper

Preparation time 45 minutes, plus 1 hour to overnight marinating time

Cooking time 15 minutes

Makes 8 small plates or servings

BUY AND ARRANGE

Raita with naan bread (see p71) • selection of chutneys and pickles (see p70) • spice-dusted shrimp (see p148)

PARTNER WITH

Coconut shrimp (see p14) • halibut parcels (see p146) • pea and shrimp samosas (see p194)

Sticky chicken wings
in teriyaki sauce

If you can, buy organic chicken—it has more flavor. The wings are easier to eat if they're cut in half, but if you don't feel confident doing this, ask the butcher to take care of it.

1 To make the teriyaki sauce, place all the ingredients in a saucepan and heat until the sugar is dissolved. Transfer to a large bowl.

2 Take each chicken wing and snap back each joint. Using a pair of poultry scissors or a cleaver, cut through the knuckle and separate into 2 pieces. Add the chicken to the teriyaki sauce, cover, and marinate overnight in the refrigerator.

3 Preheat the oven to 350°F (180°C). Remove the wings from the marinade and place them on a nonstick baking sheet. Cover with foil and roast for 30 minutes. Remove the foil and roast for another 15 minutes, until glossy and crispy at the edges.

Prepare ahead

The marinade can be made 1 week ahead and refrigerated. The wings can be marinated for up to 72 hours before cooking.

INGREDIENTS

5 lb (2.5 kg) chicken wings

Sauce

¼ cup dark soy sauce

¼ cup sake

2 tbsp mirin (rice wine)

5 tbsp sugar

½ cup apricot juice

1 tbsp grated fresh ginger

2 garlic cloves, finely chopped

1 tsp Tabasco sauce

Juice of ½ lemon

2 tbsp rice vinegar

Preparation time 15 minutes, plus marinating time

Cooking time 45 minutes

Makes 30 wings

BUY AND ARRANGE

Steamed edamame (*see p173*)
• freshly sliced watermelon (*see p215*) • shrimp and cucumber skewers (*see p149*)

PARTNER WITH

Saffron coconut soup (*see p42*)
• miso halibut bites (*see p140*)
• glass noodle salad (*see p76*)

Hainanese chicken
with soy and chili pepper dipping sauce

This recipe is based on a classic Chinese dish, which features a whole, poached bird. This is a bite-sized variation enlivened with cucumber ribbons and crunchy lettuce.

1 In a saucepan, bring the stock to a boil, add the chicken breasts, and poach for 5 minutes. Turn off the heat and place a lid on the saucepan. Leave the chicken to rest for 30 minutes.

2 Drain the chicken, transfer to a cutting board, and cut into thin slices. Using the lettuce leaves as cups, fill with the chicken, cucumber, scallions, and cilantro, and garnish with red chili pepper. Serve with the sweet soy and chili pepper dipping sauce.

Prepare ahead
The sauce can be made 1 day in advance. Kept refrigerated, the chicken can be poached earlier on the same day you serve it .

INGREDIENTS

2½ cups chicken stock

4 boneless skinless chicken breasts

20–25 heart of romaine lettuce leaves, chilled for serving

2 Lebanese or other small cucumbers, thinly sliced lengthwise

4 scallions, very thinly sliced lengthwise

1 small handful fresh cilantro leaves, roughly chopped

1 red chili pepper, thinly sliced, to garnish

1 recipe sweet soy and chili pepper dipping sauce (*see p218*), to serve

Preparation time 10 minutes

Cooking time 5 minutes, plus 30 minutes resting

Makes 20–25 small portions

BUY AND ARRANGE

Steamed edamame with sea salt (*see p173*) • spicy peanut dip (*see p71*) • fresh oysters on the shell (*see p148*)

PARTNER WITH

Crispy scallops (*see p24*) • pork and shrimp dumplings (*see p184*) • coconut macaroons (*see p210*)

Seared beef carpaccio
with mustard mint sauce and arugula

Carpaccio is simple to make at home and perfect for preparing in advance. I've suggested a larger piece of beef than you'll need because it is much easier to slice in this quantity. Use what is left over as a tasty sandwich filling.

1 Preheat a nonstick frying pan over medium-high heat. Brush the meat with 2 tablespoons of olive oil, and sprinkle with the salt and pepper. Place in the pan and brown quickly on all sides. Remove and tightly wrap with plastic wrap to create as round a shape as possible. Place in the freezer for one or two hours.

2 Meanwhile, to make the sauce, place all the ingredients in a small bowl and whisk until thoroughly combined.

3 Using a very sharp meat knife, slice the semi-frozen meat into 8 slices, about ¼ in (6 mm) thick. Place each slice between two pieces of parchment paper. Gently pound the beef with a meat tenderizer or with the side of a rolling pin, avoiding tearing. Place one slice in a shallow glass dish. Drizzle with olive oil and sprinkle with salt and coarsely ground black pepper. Repeat with the remaining slices. Refrigerate until serving time.

4 Carefully arrange the meat on a platter or on individual plates. Spoon the sauce to one side and sprinkle with capers. Garnish with the Parmesan and arugula.

Prepare ahead

Both the beef and the sauce can be prepared in the morning, covered, and kept in the refrigerator until ready to serve.

INGREDIENTS

8 oz (250 g) beef filet, trimmed of all fat and gristle

2 tbsp extra-virgin olive oil, plus extra for drizzling

½ tsp each salt and pepper, plus more as needed

1 tbsp small capers, rinsed

¼ cup thinly shaved Parmesan curls

2 large handfuls arugula leaves

Sauce

1 tbsp Dijon mustard

1 tbsp chopped mint leaves

2 tbsp extra-virgin olive oil

1 tbsp balsamic vinegar

Preparation time 20 minutes, plus 1–2 hours freezing time

Makes 8 small servings

BUY AND ARRANGE

Fig, prosciutto, and mozzarella salad (see p92) • marinated mushrooms (see p172) • marinated anchovies (see p30)

PARTNER WITH

Fried artichokes, Roman style (see p12) • spiced goat cheese balls (see p59) • creamy celery and fennel soup (see p34)

Tandoori chicken thighs
with tomato and coconut sambal

Many tandoori restaurants use food coloring in this dish. However, once you've made this homemade version, you will see that such artifice isn't necessary.

1 Cut 3 slashes across the top of each chicken thigh. Combine all of the remaining ingredients, except the sambal, in a shallow glass dish. Add the chicken, turn to coat, and marinate for at least 4 hours, but preferably overnight.

2 Preheat the oven to its highest setting. Remove the chicken from the marinade, spread on a large, nonstick baking sheet, and cook for 30 minutes, until crispy around the edges. Alternatively cook under a very hot broiler or on a barbecue grill. Serve with the tomato and coconut sambal.

Prepare ahead

The chicken should, if possible, be marinated overnight. It can be partially roasted for about 20 minutes, refrigerated, and then cooked for another 10 minutes before serving. The tomato and coconut sambal can be made 4 hours in advance.

INGREDIENTS

8 large chicken thighs with the bone in (skinless, if you prefer)

½ cup yogurt

3 garlic cloves, crushed

1 tsp garam masala

Juice of ½ lemon

1 tbsp grated fresh ginger

1 tsp ground coriander

1 tsp chili powder

1 tbsp ground cumin

1 recipe tomato and coconut sambal (*see p92*), to serve

Preparation time 10 minutes, plus 4 hours marinating time

Cooking time 30 minutes

Makes 8 thighs

BUY AND ARRANGE

Selection of chutneys and pickles (*see p70*) • unshelled pistachios (*see p31*))

PARTNER WITH

Tomato and ginger soup (*see p50*) • pea and shrimp samosas (*see p194*) • seared cinnamon duck (*see p124*)

Sage and lemon meatballs
with Parmesan

Using veal allows you to make the most featherweight, juicy meatballs, but if you don't like to use it, you can substitute ground pork instead.

1 Preheat the oven to 400°F (200°C). Place the bread in a large mixing bowl with the milk and leave to soak until softened. Add the meat, sage, fennel seed, garlic, lemon zest, tomatoes, Parmesan, egg, salt, and pepper. Mix well with your hands and shape into 1-in (2.5-cm) meatballs.

2 Heat the oil in a nonstick frying pan to medium-high. Fry the meatballs in batches of 5–6 for 5 minutes, until browned on all sides. Shake the pan frequently to keep them from sticking. Drain on paper towels and place in the oven while cooking the other batches. Serve on the radicchio leaves with the vinegar for dipping.

Prepare ahead

The meatballs can be made the day before and reheated in an oven preheated to 400°F (200°C) for 4 minutes, or until warmed through. Alternatively, they can be frozen raw or partially cooked, defrosted, then cooked before eating.

INGREDIENTS

2 slices white bread, crusts removed

¼ cup milk

1 lb (450 g) veal or pork mince

¼ cup fresh sage, finely chopped

1 tsp fennel seed, crushed

1 garlic clove, finely chopped

Grated zest of 1 lemon

2 sun-dried tomatoes in oil, finely chopped

⅔ cup Parmesan, grated

1 egg, beaten

½ tsp each salt and pepper

2 tbsp olive oil

Radicchio leaves, presoaked for 1 hour in ice water to remove bitterness, to serve

Balsamic vinegar, for dipping

Preparation time 15 minutes
Cooking time 35 minutes
Makes 35 meatballs

BUY AND ARRANGE

Radishes with tapenade (see p173) • chicory salad (see p93) • gorgonzola crostini (see p31)

PARTNER WITH

Chunky eggplant sticks (see p23) • bagna cauda (see p54) • three-tomato salad (see p86)

Five-spice hoisin ribs
with scallions

Slow cooking makes the pork wonderfully tender, nearly to the point of melting off the bones. If you prefer, ask your butcher to prepare the spare ribs for you.

1 Preheat the oven to 275°F (140°C). Rub the ribs with the five-spice powder and season to taste with salt and pepper. Divide between 2 nonstick roasting pans, cover tightly with foil, and cook for 1 hour.

2 Meanwhile, to make the sauce, heat the oil in a wok over medium-high heat until hot and add the ginger and garlic. Fry for 1 minute, then add the remaining sauce ingredients. Remove the ribs from the oven and mix well with the sauce. Return to the oven and cook, covered, for 30 minutes. Remove the foil and complete cooking for a final 30 minutes. Serve on plates, garnished with the scallions.

Prepare ahead

The ribs can be prepared ahead of time and reheated for 5 minutes in an oven preheated to 400°F (200°C).

INGREDIENTS

3½ lb (1.5 kg) pork spare ribs, cut into single ribs and halved

1 tsp five-spice powder

Salt and pepper

5 scallions, finely sliced lengthwise, to garnish

Sauce

3 tbsp peanut oil

2 tsp grated root ginger

2 garlic cloves, crushed

¼ cup hoisin sauce

2 tbsp soy sauce

2 tbsp bottled sweet chili pepper dipping sauce

¼ cup honey

⅓ cup soft light brown sugar

⅓ cup dry sherry

Preparation time 15 minutes
Cooking time 2 hours
Makes about 30 ribs

BUY AND ARRANGE

Watercress salad (see p93) • roasted asparagus with soy (see p172) • selection of sushi (see p31)

PARTNER WITH

Thai corn fritters (see p26) • glass noodle salad (see p76) • avocado crostini (see p164)

No need to be shy; cooking fish and seafood isn't as scary as you might think. Find some exceptionally fresh fish, a fish counter with knowledgeable staff, and you are all set. Steamed, roasted, grilled, or sushi-style, eating fish is always a delicate and special pleasure.

Fish

Baby clams
with caramelized onions and oloroso sherry

Oloroso is a dry, raisin-scented sherry with a slightly smoky taste. It is wonderful to cook with as well as to sip chilled. Cockles may be used instead of baby clams in this recipe.

1 To draw out any sand from inside the clams, soak them fully immersed in cold water with a handful of salt for 30 minutes. Rinse the clams, wrap in a wet dish towel, place in a bowl, and refrigerate until using. Discard any clams with open shells.

2 Heat the oil in a medium-sized saucepan over medium-high heat, add the onions, salt, and pepper, and sauté for 10–12 minutes, until the onions are caramelized. Add the garlic and ham, and sauté for an additional 3 minutes, until soft. Stir in the sherry and cook for 1–2 minutes.

3 Just before serving, add the clams to the pan: they should open in about 1–2 minutes. Discard any that do not open. Sprinkle with parsley and serve with crostini.

Prepare ahead

The sauce may be prepared ahead of time, and the prepared clams added and cooked just before serving.

INGREDIENTS

2 lb (1 kg) baby clams, cleaned and beards removed

3 tbsp olive oil

2 yellow onions, finely sliced

½ tsp each salt and pepper

2 garlic cloves, finely chopped

6 slices serrano ham or proscuitto, chopped

½ cup oloroso or manzanilla sherry

Small handful flat-leaf parsley leaves, finely chopped

8 slices sourdough bread, toasted, rubbed with garlic and olive oil, to serve

Preparation time 10 minutes, plus soaking

Cooking time 20 minutes

Makes 8 small bowls of clams

BUY AND ARRANGE

Radicchio, orange, and arugula salad (see p92) • roasted garlic with warm bread (see p71) • pan-fried chorizo (see p149)

PARTNER WITH

Pan-fried halloumi salad (see p82) • fried artichokes, Roman style (see p12) • chocolate Frangelico pudding (see p200)

Seared sesame tuna
with sweet soy and chili dressing

Making seared rare tuna is very easy. Just be sure to buy good-quality fish—ruby red with a little white marbling throughout—and do not overcook it.

1 Cut the tuna lengthwise into 2–3 long slices, 2 in (5 cm) wide, like small beef filets. Heat a large, nonstick sauté pan on medium-high heat. Meanwhile, rub the tuna filets with the olive oil and then roll them in the salt, pepper, and sesame seeds. Place the filets in the dry pan and sear until brown on all sides. Be sure not to overcook—the meat should be rare inside.

2 Allow the tuna to cool slightly, then wrap very tightly in plastic wrap. The more tightly it is wrapped, the firmer it will be to slice. Refrigerate for at least 1 hour and preferably overnight.

3 Unwrap the fish and slice very thinly, about ¼ in (5 mm) thick. Arrange a bed of scallions, apple, and cucumber on individual plates, and top with the tuna. Serve accompanied by the sweet soy and chili pepper dressing.

Prepare ahead

The fish is best prepared the night before so that it is very firm to cut. The dressing can be made and the vegetables and fruit sliced on the morning of serving day. Keep the onions and apples in ice water to prevent discoloring, and drain before serving.

INGREDIENTS

1½ lb (750 g) fresh tuna, preferably tail

1 tbsp olive oil

½ tsp each salt and pepper

1 tsp each black sesame seeds and white sesame seeds

4 scallions, cut into matchsticks

1 Granny Smith, or any apple, cut into matchsticks

1 cucumber, cut into matchsticks

1 recipe sweet soy and chili pepper dressing (see p218), to serve

Preparation time 15 minutes, plus 1–12 hours refrigeration for the tuna

Cooking time 5 minutes

Makes 8 small appetizers

BUY AND ARRANGE

Watercress salad with spring onion (see p93) • crab and cream cheese dip (see p71) • mango fool (see p215)

PARTNER WITH

Peking seared duck rolls (see p180) • sticky chicken wings (see p126) • avocado crostini (see p164)

Halibut bites
with sticky miso glaze

Other fish, such as scallops, monkfish, or firm cod filets, can be used instead. The saltiness of the light miso paste preserves the fish while marinating.

1 To make the glaze, mix the mirin, miso paste, sake, and sugar in a small bowl. Add the fish and turn to coat thoroughly. Cover and leave to marinate in the refrigerator for at least 24 hours.

2 Preheat the broiler to medium. Place the fish on a roasting tray with a flat rack. Broil for 4–5 minutes, until golden and crispy around the edges. Sprinkle with the scallions and serve warm with chopsticks or toothpicks.

Prepare ahead
The fish can be marinated 24–48 hours before serving. It should be broiled just before serving and eaten immediately.

INGREDIENTS

1 lb (450 g) halibut, cleaned of all gristle and cut into 1½-in (4-cm) chunks

3 scallions, with green stems, sliced lengthwise

Glaze
⅓ cup mirin (rice wine)
⅔ cup light miso paste
3 tbsp sake
½ cup superfine sugar

Preparation time 15 minutes plus 24 hours marinating time
Cooking time 5 minutes
Makes about 30 bites

BUY AND ARRANGE

Shrimp and cucumber skewers (*see p149*) • crab and cream cheese dip (*see p71*) • watercress salad with scallions (*see p93*)

PARTNER WITH

Roasted butternut squash (*see p162*) • crispy scallops (*see p24*) • seared sesame tuna (*see p138*)

Grilled butterfly shrimp
with butter, lime, and jalapeño

Cooking shrimp with their shells on keeps them succulent and juicy. Not only do larger shrimp look more impressive, but it is also easier to butterfly them.

1 Using a very sharp knife, cut each shrimp through the shell on the back (outside curve). Don't cut all the way through, but just enough to split the shrimp open. This is butterflying. Rinse under cold water to remove any veins. Drain on paper towels.

2 Heat the broiler to medium. Place the shrimp in a shallow baking dish and pour on the butter and oil. Sprinkle with the garlic, chipotle, jalapeño, salt, and pepper. Cook under the broiler for 1–2 minutes, or until the shrimp just turn pink. Sprinkle with the lime juice, zest, and fresh cilantro and serve immediately with the lime halves.

Prepare ahead

The butter can be mixed with the chili peppers 2 days in advance, refrigerated, and melted before cooking. The shrimp can be butterflied the night before and refrigerated.

INGREDIENTS

1 lb (450 g) large shrimp in shells

2 tbsp unsalted butter, melted

2 tbsp extra-virgin olive oil

2 garlic cloves, crushed

1 chipotle chili pepper in adobo, deseeded and chopped (or extra jalapeño)

1 jalapeño or other green chili pepper, deseeded and minced

½ tsp each salt and pepper

Juice of 1 large lime

1 tsp lime zest

3 tbsp chopped fresh cilantro

2 limes, halved, to serve

Preparation time 25 minutes
Cooking time 2 minutes
Makes about 20–24 shrimp

BUY AND ARRANGE

Palm heart and avocado salad (*see p92*) • sweet potato wedges (*see p172*) • baby lettuce with walnut oil and sherry vinegar (*see p92*)

PARTNER WITH

Crab and Gruyère nachos (*see p142*) • soft-shell steak tacos (*see p178*) • chili pepper gazpacho (*see p36*)

Crab and Gruyère nachos
with charred tomato salsa

A plate of nachos rarely sits uneaten. There's something irresistible about melted cheese. Instead of the chipotle, you can use another red chili or jalapeño pepper.

1 To make the salsa, place the garlic cloves and peppers in a nonstick frying pan and dry-fry over medium-high heat, stirring, until blackened on all sides. Remove from the heat and set the garlic aside. Place the peppers in a resealable plastic bag, seal, and leave for 5 minutes to steam. Scrape off the skins and take the seeds out. Peel the cooled garlic.

2 Meanwhile, heat the broiler to high. Spread out the tomatoes and onion on a large, nonstick baking sheet and broil for 6–7 minutes, until blackened. Transfer to a food processor with the garlic, peppers, chipotle in adobo, if using, and the cilantro and salt. Pulse until you have a coarse-textured puree. Transfer to a bowl and add the lime juice and extra salt to taste, if necessary.

3 Preheat the oven to 400°F (200°C). Spread the tortilla chips out on a baking sheet. Sprinkle with the crab, pickled jalapeño, onion, and cheese. Bake for 6 minutes, until the cheese is melted. Serve immediately with the salsa.

Prepare ahead

The vegetables and cheese can be chopped and grated in the morning. The nachos can be assembled 1 hour before baking.

INGREDIENTS

½-lb (200-g) bag good quality corn tortilla chips

8 oz (250 g) cooked fresh white crab meat

1 pickled jalapeño pepper, very thinly sliced

1 small red onion, finely diced

8 oz (250 g) finely grated Gruyère or sharp cheddar

Salsa

4 garlic cloves, unpeeled

2 jalapeño or other small green chili peppers

1 lb (500 g) ripe plum tomatoes

1 red onion, thickly sliced

1 chipotle in adobo, deseeded (*optional*)

Small handful fresh cilantro

½ tsp salt

Juice of 1 lime

Preparation time 20 minutes
Cooking time 16 minutes
Makes 8 servings

BUY AND ARRANGE	PARTNER WITH
Watermelon and feta salad (*see p93*) • piquillo peppers with sherry vinegar (*see p172*) • Spanish deli plate (*see p30*)	Soft shell steak tacos (*see p178*) • baby clams (*see p136*) • chili-pepper gazpacho (*see p36*) • chocolate cupcakes (*see p202*)

Smoked trout carpaccio
with pink peppercorns and dill

You can make this with any thinly sliced smoked fish. Instead of trout, try smoked salmon, tuna, or swordfish, but leave the job of cutting it to the professionals at the fish store.

1 Divide the fish slices between individual plates and drizzle with the olive oil. Sprinkle with the fennel, onion, peppercorns, capers, and dill.

2 Just before serving, spoon some crème fraîche over the fish and place some arugula and a lemon or lime wedge on each plate.

Prepare ahead

This dish can be made, covered with plastic wrap, and refrigerated for several hours before serving.

INGREDIENTS

8 oz (250 g) smoked trout slices

2 tbsp extra-virgin olive oil

⅓ fennel bulb, core removed and finely diced

1 small red onion, finely diced

2 tbsp pink peppercorns, crushed

1 tbsp tiny capers

Small bunch fresh chopped dill, stems removed

½ cup crème fraîche or sour cream

Small handful arugula

Lemons or limes, quartered, to serve

Preparation time 15 minutes
Makes 8 small plates

BUY AND ARRANGE

Chicory salad (*see p93*) • gorgonzola crostini (*see p31*) • biscotti with mascarpone and dessert wine (*see p215*)

PARTNER WITH

Mushroom and chestnut soup (*see p38*) • rosemary lamb chops (*see p118*) • baby beets and bresaola (*see p168*)

Roasted shrimp and tomatoes
with gremolata

Butterflying shrimp creates a more elegant presentation and prevents them from curling. Have plenty of crusty bread available to soak up this delicious sauce.

1 Preheat the oven to 350°F (180°C). Place the tomatoes, cut side up, on a baking tray, and sprinkle with the garlic, chilli peppers, olive oil, salt, and pepper. Bake for 20 minutes.

2 Remove the tomatoes from the oven and add the shrimp, fennel seed, and lemon juice. Heat the broiler to medium and broil the shrimp and tomato mixture for 4–5 minutes, until the shrimp turn white. Divide between individual plates, sprinkle with the parsley and lemon zest, and serve warm or at room temperature.

Prepare ahead
The tomatoes can be roasted, and the other ingredients chopped, on the same day you serve them. If serving at room temperature, the dish can be fully made 2 hours before.

INGREDIENTS

½ lb (250 g) baby or very small plum tomatoes, halved

2 garlic cloves, finely chopped

½ tsp crushed, dried red chili peppers

4 tbsp extra-virgin olive oil

½ tsp each salt and pepper

1 lb (450 g) shrimp, peeled, deveined, and butterflied (see p141)

½ tsp fennel seed, crushed

Juice and grated zest of 1 lemon

3 tbsp flat-leaf parsley, finely chopped

Preparation time 10 minutes
Cooking time 5 minutes
Makes 8 servings

BUY AND ARRANGE

Pesto and aioli with grissini breadsticks (see p70) • marinated anchovies (see p30) • pan-fried padron peppers (see p30)

PARTNER WITH

Farro salad (see p78) • artichoke puff pastry bites (see p196) • strawberries and figs (see p207)

Halibut parcels
with cilantro and coconut chutney

Find the freshest, preferably organic, coconuts to use in this recipe. However, quality dried coconut can still be amazingly good. Try salmon or sea bass in the recipe instead.

1 Preheat the oven to 400°F (200°C). To make the chutney, heat a small, nonstick frying pan over medium-high heat, add the cumin seeds, and dry-toast while stirring. Cool and grind in a spice mill or mortar. Reserve a little cilantro as a garnish, and place the remainder in a food processor or blender with the garlic, ginger, jalapeño, and lemon juice. Process to a paste. Transfer to a small bowl and stir in the coconut, toasted cumin seeds, and sugar.

2 Cut 8 large pieces of foil. Put a small pat of the butter on each piece. Top with 2 tbsp of chutney, then a piece of fish, and finally another 2 tbsp chutney, then season with salt and pepper. Fold the foil around the fish to create sealed packets, place on a baking sheet, and bake in the oven for 10 minutes, or until the fish is tender and can be pierced with a knife. Open the packets, garnish with the reserved cilantro, and serve with lemon wedges.

Prep ahead

If you keep them refrigerated, the parcels and chutney can be made a few hours before serving

INGREDIENTS

1½ lb (750 g) halibut, skinned, boned, cut into 8 pieces

4 tbsp unsalted butter

Salt and pepper, to taste

1 lemon, cut into wedges

Chutney

1 tsp cumin seeds

Large bunch fresh cilantro

2 garlic cloves

1-in (2½-cm) piece fresh ginger, peeled and sliced

1 jalapeño, seeded and chopped

Juice of 2 lemons

1 cup grated fresh or dried unsweetened coconut (organic if possible)

2 tsp sugar

Preparation time 15 minutes
Cooking time 10 minutes
Makes 8 parcels

BUY AND ARRANGE

Selection of chutneys and pickles (see p70) • raita with naan bread (see p71) • spice-dusted shrimp (see p148)

PARTNER WITH

Tomato and ginger soup (see p50) • crispy vegetable pakoras (see p20) • strawberries and figs (see p207)

Quick fish and meat
buy-and-arrange ideas for quick-to-prepare dishes

Fish and meat dishes are considered to be complicated and tricky to make, but there are some clever shortcuts that will save you time. Fresh fish needs little added to it, and tastes wonderful with just a little lemon juice or salt and pepper. Chorizo and merguez sausages are simply pan-fried—and impossible to resist.

Fresh crab crostini

Toast 16 small slices of French or sourdough bread and brush each with some olive oil. In a bowl, mix together ½ lb (225 g) fresh cooked white crab meat, the juice of half a lemon, a pinch of crushed chili, 2 tablespoons extra-virgin olive oil, and some salt and pepper. Top each crostini with a good portion of the crab mixture.

Spice-dusted shrimp

Butterfly 16 large, peeled shrimp by slicing a deep cut down the back and opening them out flat. Rinse under water. Place either some ground fennel, ground cumin, ground coriander, or sumac in a bowl. Dip each shrimp into the bowl to fully coat then season with salt and pepper. Heat 1 tablespoon olive oil in a nonstick frying pan over medium heat and fry the shrimp until just opaque, about 3 minutes. Serve on a platter.

Smoked salmon blinis

Buy some ready-made blinis and bake them until crisp in a moderately hot oven. Top each blini with some small strips of smoked salmon, a few capers, a spoonful of crème fraîche, some finely diced red onion, and a little freshly chopped dill. Serve them on a platter.

Fresh oysters on the shell

Ask the fish counter to open the oysters for you, or if you wish to open them yourself, be sure to use the right knife and gloves. Place the oysters, still in their opened shell, on a bed of ice on a small tray and serve them with some Tabasco sauce and lemon wedges for guests to add as they wish. Alternatively, in a small serving bowl, mix together 5 tablespoons rice wine vinegar with 1 small diced chili pepper and allow guests to sprinkle about ½ teaspoon of the mixture over their oyster before eating.

Tuna tartare on cucumber slices

In a bowl, combine ¼ lb (125 g) finely diced raw tuna with 1 teaspoon lime juice, ½ teaspoon wasabi, and 1 teaspoon soy sauce. Thinly slice 1 medium cucumber and serve 1 heaped teaspoon of the tuna mixture on each slice.

Gravlax and mustard dill sauce

Buy some quality gravlax salmon from a delicatessen or supermarket. In a bowl, mix 4 tablespoons Dijon mustard, 1 teaspoon sugar, 1 tablespoon chopped dill, and 1 tablespoon white wine vinegar. Serve the gravlax with the dip and some toasted dark or seeded bread.

Shrimp and cucumber skewers

Cut 1 medium cucumber into ¾-in (2-cm) cubes. Thread 1 large cooked shrimp and 1 cucumber cube onto each skewer. Alternatively, use slender forks or toothpicks. Serve the skewers with a bowl of hoisin sauce or ketchup manis, also known as Indonesian sweet soy, to dip.

Pan-fried chorizo

Cut some chorizo into ½-in (1.5-cm) pieces or buy smaller chorizos and use them whole. Heat a little olive oil in a nonstick frying pan until hot. Add the chorizo to the pan and fry until crispy, about 2 minutes. Remove with a slotted spoon and drain on paper towels, then serve.

Five-spice chicken breast bites

Cut 3 skinless, boneless chicken breasts into 1-in (2.5-cm) pieces. Place some five-spice powder in a bowl. Roll the chicken pieces in the powder, then season with salt. Heat 1 tbsp vegetable oil in a nonstick pan and brown the chicken on all sides, about 5 minutes. Serve with lime wedges, chili pepper dipping sauce, and some toothpicks to pick them up.

Baby shrimp with arugula

Place ½ lb (225 g) small, cooked shrimp on a serving dish. Sprinkle with 2 large handfuls chopped arugula and drizzle with 1 tablespoon extra-virgin olive oil. Serve with lemon wedges.

Shrimp and cucumber skewers

Pan-fried Merguez lamb sausages

Heat 1 tablespoon olive oil over medium-high heat in a nonstick frying pan until hot. Add the sausages and pan-fry, turning occasionally, until golden and cooked through. Slice the sausages into smaller pieces and serve with toothpicks.

Thai shrimp

In a large bowl, place some large, cooked and peeled shrimp, about ½ lb (225 g), 4 tbsp sweet chili pepper dipping sauce, and 1 small handful chopped fresh cilantro, and mix well to coat the shrimp. Serve them on small skewers or with toothpicks for guests to help themselves.

Choice is not an issue with fresh vegetables. From fall's crimson beets to spring's emerald asparagus, each season brings a rich new selection. There are endless ways to prepare them, and simple is often best. Usually, all that's called for is a hint of garlic, seasoning, lemon juice, or creamy goat cheese.

Vegetables

Serrano-rolled asparagus
with saffron aioli

Tasty on its own or divine with a dipping sauce, this undemanding asparagus dish works well for Mediterranean and Moorish menus.

1 Bring a saucepan of salted water to a boil, add the asparagus, and simmer for 1–2 minutes. Remove with tongs, and immediately plunge into ice water to retain color and halt cooking. Drain on a dish towel.

2 Roll two spears of asparagus in one piece of ham. Repeat with the remaining asparagus and ham. Refrigerate until ready to serve with the saffron aioli.

Prepare ahead

The asparagus can be blanched and rolled on the morning of serving day, then covered with parchment paper and then plastic wrap. The aioli can be made the day before. Both should be refrigerated.

INGREDIENTS

2 bunches asparagus, ends trimmed

12 slices serrano ham, bresaola, or prosciutto, cut in half

1 recipe saffron lemon aioli (*see p217*), to serve

Preparation time 20 minutes
Cooking time 2 minutes
Makes 24 asparagus

BUY AND ARRANGE

Baby lettuces with sherry vinegar (*see p92*) • sweet potato wedges (*see p172*) • hummus with smoky paprika (*see p70*)

PARTNER WITH

Citrus swordfish brochettes (*see p96*) • garbanzo and chili pepper dip (*see p68*) • chili pepper gazpacho (*see p36*)

Wild mushroom crostini
with mascarpone and sherry vinegar

When making the crostini, try to bake the bread until it is browned at the edges but still chewy in the center.

1 Preheat the oven to 400°F (200°C). Place the bread on a nonstick baking sheet, brush with the oil, and sprinkle with salt. Bake for 6 minutes. Rub the bread with the whole garlic clove, then chop the clove for the topping and leave the bread to cool.

2 For the topping, heat the oil in a pan over medium-high heat and sauté the garlic for 1 minute. Add mushrooms and salt, tossing gently to coat. Sauté for 4 minutes, or until just wilting. Add the vinegar and parsley, toss gently, and remove from heat. Spread 1 tablespoon of mascarpone on each crostini, spoon on the mushroom mixture, and sprinkle with zest.

Prepare ahead

Store toasted crostini in an airtight container 2 days ahead. Sauté mushrooms and refrigerate 2 hours before serving. Reheat or bring to room temperature and make crostini up to ½ hour before serving.

INGREDIENTS

16 slices sourdough, ciabatta, or other artisan bread

3 tbsp extra-virgin olive oil

Topping

3 tbsp extra-virgin olive oil

2 garlic cloves, peeled and 1 finely chopped

1 lb (450 g) mixed wild mushrooms, such as trompettes de la mort or chanterelles, quartered or thickly sliced

¼ tsp salt

1 tbsp sherry vinegar

Small handful flat-leaf parsley, finely chopped

8 oz (225 g) mascarpone cheese

Finely grated zest of 1 orange

Preparation time 25 minutes
Cooking time 11 minutes
Serves 16 pieces

BUY AND ARRANGE

Palm heart and avocado salad (see p92) • roasted peppers with garlic (see p172) • Italian deli plate (see p30)

PARTNER WITH

Spinach and peppered pear salad (see p84)• Sicilian artichoke bottoms (see p154) • raspberry meringues (see p208)

Sicilian artichoke bottoms
with provolone and capers

Preparing an artichoke bottom is easier than with hearts, which require more effort. Any type of bread is fine for the topping, but I find sourdough works well.

1 Preheat the oven to 400°F (200°C). Peel the outer leaves off one artichoke until you reach the pale green, soft part. Slice off the stem. Using a heavy, sharp knife, cut away the top three-quarters of the artichoke, reserving the bottom. Trim off the hard edges with a smaller paring knife. Using a spoon, scrape out any remaining inner choke. Place the artichoke in a bowl of water with a third of the lemon juice. Repeat with the other artichokes.

2 Add 2 chopped garlic cloves and 3 tablespoons of the oil to a very large saucepan over medium-high heat and sauté the garlic until slightly golden. Drain the artichokes, add to the pan, and cook for 1 minute, then add the mint, ½ teaspoon each of salt and pepper, the water, and the remaining lemon juice. Reduce the heat to medium-low and cover the saucepan. Cook the artichokes for 10 minutes or until they can be pierced with a knife, but are not mushy. Remove and place on a nonstick baking sheet.

3 In a small bowl, combine the breadcrumbs, lemon zest, parsley, capers, and the remaining garlic, olive oil, salt, and pepper. Place one slice of cheese on each artichoke bottom and distribute the breadcrumb mixture evenly on top of each. Bake in the oven for 15 minutes or until the cheese has melted and the breadcrumbs are toasty. Serve warm, garnished with the zest and arugula sprigs.

Prepare ahead
The artichokes can be trimmed and poached the day before, then covered and refrigerated. The topping can also be made the day before and kept in the refrigerator.

INGREDIENTS

6–8 globe artichokes

Juice of 3 lemons

4 garlic cloves, chopped

6 tbsp olive oil

3 tbsp chopped fresh mint

1 tsp each salt and pepper

4 tbsp water

1 cup homemade breadcrumbs

1 tsp grated lemon zest

3 tsp finely chopped flat-leaf parsley

1 tbsp small capers, rinsed

2 oz (50 g) or 6–8 slices of provolone cheese

Pared lemon zest, to garnish

Arugula, to garnish

Preparation time 45 minutes
Cooking time 25 minutes
Makes 6–8 bites

BUY AND ARRANGE

Radicchio, orange, and arugula salad (see p92) • prosciutto-wrapped melon (see p31) • marinated anchovies (see p30)

PARTNER WITH

Orange and beet soup (see p40) • three-tomato salad (see p86) • seared beef carpaccio (see p128)

Colors
- Magenta pink
- Silver and gold
- Warm tangerine
- Rich purple
- Crimson red

Tableware
- Mixed styles of metal bowls
- Silk tablecloths
- Small wooden spice bowls
- Distressed metal cutlery
- Scattered rose petals

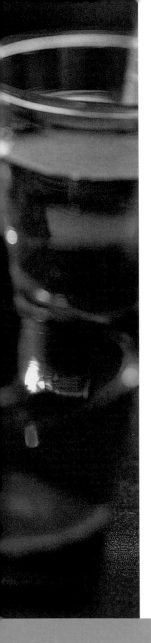

Bollywood nights

Indian cuisine is about glamor; redolent with heady spices, creamy with the texture of coconut, and brightened by the taste of sweet mango. Unique for the many fried snacks served with refreshing yogurt dips, Indian food is a delight for your senses.

Garlic, fresh cilantro, and ginger form the base of most dishes, and it is a great combination. Cardamom, cumin, and coriander may already be familiar spices, but there are more. Once you are exposed to the fascinating taste of amchoor, you'll understand the real meaning of exotic. Made from ground dried mango, amchoor adds a gentle sour note to samosas and other foods. Boredom will never be an issue when exploring this cuisine; there is so much to discover.

When setting the table, imagine colorful saris of magenta, orange, and silver. Don't try to be quietly tasteful; think electric bright colors—beige definitely does not belong here. Metal serving dishes and wooden spice bowls add an authentic touch, if you have them. Light some candles for atmosphere and prepare to feast.

Flavors

- Spicy chili pepper
- Fresh cilantro
- Sweet garlic
- Sour amchoor
- Fragrant turmeric

Nibbles

- Raita with naan bread (*see p71*)
- Chutneys and pickles (*see p70*)
- Crispy vegetable pakoras (*see p20*)
- Sugar-coated fennel seeds (*see p215*)
- Tomato and coconut sambal (*see p92*)

Menu

Seared cinnamon duck
with mango chutney and poppadoms

Coconut shrimp
with mango mint dipping sauce

Tomato and ginger soup
with spiced oil

Crispy vegetable pakoras with
tamarind and ginger dipping sauce

Tandoori chicken thighs
with tomato and coconut sambal

Raspberry meringues
with white chocolate swirls

BUY AND ARRANGE

Raita with naan bread
(see p71)

Selection of chutneys and pickles
with mini poppadoms (see p70)

Exotic fruit salad
(see p215)

Seared cinnamon duck
(see p124)

Coconut shrimp
(see p14)

Tomato and ginger soup
(see p50)

Crispy vegetable pakoras
(see p20)

Tandoori chicken thighs
(see p130)

Raspberry meringues
(see p208)

The night before
- Marinate duck breasts
- Make mango chutney
- Make tomato and ginger soup
- Marinate tandoori chicken
- Make raspberry meringues

In the morning
- Sear duck breasts
- Make mango mint sauce
- Make tamarind and ginger sauce
- Whip cream and chop nuts for meringues
- Make iced chai tea
- Make raita

Four hours before
- Make crispy vegetable pakoras
- Roast tandoori chicken thighs
- Make tomato and coconut sambal
- Make exotic fruit salad

Iced chai tea with rose petals

This tea can be made into an alcoholic cocktail by adding a measure of vanilla vodka or brandy to each glass.

INGREDIENTS

2 quarts (2 liters) boiling water

2 tbsp sugar

1 tsp rose water

8 chai tea bags

Ice

4 cinnamon sticks (*optional*)

Fresh red rose petals, to garnish

Makes 8 iced chai teas

Pour the boiling water into a large pitcher, then add the sugar, rose water, and tea bags. Let steep for 5 minutes, then remove the bags. Add some ice to cool the tea down. Fill each glass with more ice, pour the tea in, and add a cinnamon stick, if using. Scatter rose petals over the glasses and pitcher to garnish.

One hour before
- Coat coconut shrimp
- Reheat soup and make spiced oil

At the last minute
- Plate coconut shrimp with mango mint sauce
- Pour soup with spiced oil
- Reheat pakoras; plate with tamarind dipping sauce
- Plate raspberry meringues
- Pour iced chai tea
- Plate exotic fruit salad

Half an hour before
- Roast duck breasts; plate with chutney and poppadoms
- Fry coconut shrimp
- Reheat tandoori chicken; plate
- Plate chutneys and pickles with mini poppadoms
- Plate raita with naan bread

Rolled zucchini ribbons
with mint, chili pepper, and goat cheese

Small zucchini have a sweet, buttery taste and their flesh is tender, making it easier to create ribbons. Secure the rolls with toothpicks instead of chives if you prefer.

1 Heat the broiler to high. Using a very sharp knife, cut the zucchini into 20 lengthwise slices, about ¼ in (5 mm) thick. Brush the slices with 2 tablespoons of the olive oil and sprinkle with the salt and pepper. Put them in a broiler pan and cook on both sides until the zucchini have grill stripes. Be careful not to overcook or they will break apart when rolling. Set aside to cool.

2 Heat the remaining oil in a frying pan over medium-high heat, add the chili peppers, and fry until crisp around the edges. Drain on paper towels.

3 Bring a small saucepan of water to a boil, drop in the chives, and remove immediately with a slotted spoon. Place in cold water briefly, then leave to dry on paper towels. This prevents them from breaking during tying.

4 Spread each zucchini slice with about 1 teaspoon of goat cheese. Place a couple of mint leaves, 2–3 chili pepper slivers, and some arugula across one end so that they protrude. Gently roll the slice up and secure with a toothpick. Tie a chive around the roll and trim the ends with scissors. Remove the toothpicks and refrigerate until serving.

Prepare ahead

The zucchini can be grilled and the chili peppers sautéed—and then refrigerated—on the morning before serving them. The rolls can be prepared 2 hours ahead. To prevent sogginess, cover the rolls with paper towels and plastic wrap.

INGREDIENTS

4–5 small zucchini

3 tbsp extra-virgin olive oil

½ tsp each salt and pepper

2 thumb-sized red chili peppers, deseeded and thinly sliced

Small bunch of fresh chives

4 oz (100 g) mild goat cheese

Handful fresh mint leaves

2 small handfuls baby arugula, long stems trimmed

Toothpicks, to secure

Preparation time 20 minutes
Cooking time 10–15 minutes
Makes 20 rolls

BUY AND ARRANGE

Avocado with balsamic vinegar (*see p173*) • white bean dip (*see p71*) • brownies with chocolate sauce (*see p214*)

PARTNER WITH

Spinach and yogurt dip (*see p66*) • cumin lamb skewers (*see p112*) • spinach and peppered pear salad (*see p84*)

Roasted pepper and mozzarella
with warm anchovy agrodulce dressing

If you are short on time, use peppadews instead of roasting the peppers yourself. These sweet and sour pickled baby peppers work fantastically with the mild cheese.

1 Preheat the broiler to high. Place the peppers, skin side up, on a nonstick baking tray, and cook under the broiler for 5 minutes, until blackened. Transfer to a sealed plastic bag for 5 minutes, then remove and peel. Cut into 1-in (2.5-cm) wide strips and set aside.

2 To make the dressing, place the oil in a small sauté pan, add the garlic and anchovy, and gently fry until golden. Add the vinegar, chili peppers, honey, onion, salt, and pepper, and simmer the mixture for 2–3 minutes, until syrupy.

3 Tear the mozzarella into pieces. Divide the mozzarella and pepper among individual plates or on a platter. Drizzle with the warm dressing and sprinkle with the mint and basil leaves.

Prepare ahead
The peppers can be prepared the day before, and refrigerated. The dressing can be made several hours before serving and warmed through before using.

INGREDIENTS

6 red peppers, deseeded and quartered

3 fresh buffalo mozzarella balls, drained

Small handful fresh basil and mint leaves

Dressing

⅓ cup extra-virgin olive oil

2 garlic cloves, thinly sliced

1 anchovy, rinsed

⅛ cup red wine vinegar

½ tsp crushed red chili peppers

1½ tsp honey

1 small red onion, thinly sliced

½ tsp each salt and pepper

Preparation time 20 minutes

Cooking time 5 minutes

Makes 8 small plates, 4 appetizers, or a platter

BUY AND ARRANGE

Crushed feta dip (see p70) • spice-dusted shrimp (see p148) • biscotti, mascarpone, and dessert wine (see p215)

PARTNER WITH

Fried artichokes, Roman style (see p12) • sage and lemon meatballs (see p131)

Roasted butternut squash
with soy balsamic dressing

Butternut squash becomes sweet and creamy when roasted and shows a surprising affinity with strong Asian ingredients such as soy sauce.

1 Preheat the oven to 400°F (200°C). Place the squash on a baking sheet and drizzle with the olive oil, salt, and pepper. Bake for 20 minutes, shaking the tray a few times to prevent sticking. Remove from the oven and set aside.

2 Place the dressing ingredients in a jar, close the lid, and shake well. Place the arugula on the plates and arrange the squash on top. Pour on the dressing and top with sesame seeds, scallions, and cilantro leaves.

Prepare ahead

The butternut squash and dressing can be made on the morning of serving day. Undercook the squash and then reheat before serving. Serve within half an hour of dressing.

INGREDIENTS

1 large butternut squash, peeled, deseeded, and cut into 1-in (2.5-cm) cubes

2 tbsp olive oil

1 tsp each sea salt and pepper

4 large handfuls arugula

1 tsp toasted sesame seeds

4 scallions, finely sliced

Small handful fresh cilantro

Dressing

6 tbsp extra virgin olive oil

3 tbsp balsamic vinegar

1 tbsp soy sauce

1 medium-size red chili pepper, deseeded and finely chopped

½ garlic clove, finely chopped

1 tsp honey

Juice of ½ lime

Preparation time 15 minutes
Cooking time 20 minutes
Makes 8 small salads or 4 appetizers

BUY AND ARRANGE

Watercress salad (see p93) • shrimp and cucumber skewers (see p149) • fresh unpeeled lychees (see p215)

PARTNER WITH

Pork and shrimp dumplings (see p184) • avocado crostini (see p164)

Avocado crostini
with cream cheese and sweet chili peppers

Although it may seem strange to mix avocado with Asian flavors, chili peppers are actually magnificent when juxtaposed with creamy-flavored ingredients.

1 Preheat the oven to 400°F (200°C). To make the crostini, place the bread slices on a nonstick baking sheet. Brush with 3 tablespoons of oil, and season. Bake for 6 minutes, until browned on the edges but chewy in the center. Rub with the garlic and set the crostini aside.

2 Spread the crostini with 1–2 teaspoons of cream cheese. Top with 2 slices of avocado, then scallions. Drizzle with the sweet chili pepper dipping sauce, sprinkle with the chili peppers, and serve.

Prepare ahead

The bread slices can be prepared 2 days before, and stored in an airtight container. The crostini can be assembled half an hour before serving, but squeeze a little lemon or lime juice over the avocado to prevent browning.

INGREDIENTS

16 2-in (5-cm) square slices sourdough baguette or other chewy bread

3 tbsp olive oil

Salt and pepper, to taste

1 garlic clove, peeled

8 oz (200 g) cream cheese

4 avocado halves, each cut into 4 slices

4 scallions, finely chopped

1 recipe sweet chili and coriander dipping sauce (*see p218*), or bottled, to drizzle

2 thumb-sized red chili peppers, deseeded and thinly sliced

Preparation time 10 minutes
Cooking time 6 minutes
Makes 16 crostini

BUY AND ARRANGE

Asian cucumber salad (*see p93*) • spicy peanut dip (*see p71*) • shrimp and cucumber skewers (*see p149*)

PARTNER WITH

Red curry pumpkin soup (*see p46*) • glass noodle salad (*see p76*) • coconut macaroons (*see p210*)

Gorgonzola crostini
with seared garlic greens and raisins

Blanching greens before searing keeps their color bright and removes any potential bitterness. Any other bread, such as ciabatta, can be used in place of the sourdough.

1 To make the crostini, preheat the oven to 400°F (200°C). Place the bread slices on a nonstick baking sheet and brush with 3 tablespoons of the oil. Sprinkle with half of the salt and some black pepper. Bake for 6 minutes, until browned on the edges but still chewy in the center. Rub the bread with one of the garlic cloves and set aside.

2 Bring some salted water to a boil, add the kale, then reduce the heat and simmer for about 5 minutes or until cooked but firm. Drain and immediately plunge into ice water to preserve the color and stop the cooking. Drain again, pressing out as much water as possible with your hands, and set aside.

3 Finely slice the garlic cloves. Heat the remaining oil in a large frying pan over medium heat. Add the garlic and chili peppers, and brown lightly. Add the drained kale and toss to combine the flavors. Stir in the raisins, pine nuts, and vinegar. Toss again to heat through.

4 Spread the Gorgonzola thickly over the crostini. Spoon on the kale mixture, garnish with the Parmesan shavings, and serve.

Prepare ahead

The crostini can be made 2 days in advance and stored in an airtight container. If refrigerated, the greens can be cooked earlier on the same day you serve them, but don't toss with the remaining ingredients until 1 hour before serving, to retain the green color.

INGREDIENTS

16 thin slices sourdough bread

6 tbsp extra-virgin olive oil

1 tsp salt

Freshly ground black pepper

2 garlic cloves, peeled

4 large handfuls curly kale or other greens, chopped into 1-in (2.5-cm) pieces

½ tsp crushed dried red chili peppers

1 tbsp raisins, soaked in warm water for 10 minutes

2 tbsp pine nuts, toasted

3 tbsp balsamic vinegar

4 oz (100 g) Gorgonzola

Parmesan shavings, to garnish

Preparation time 15 minutes
Cooking time 12 minutes
Makes 16 crostini

BUY AND ARRANGE

Baby shrimp with arugula (*see p149*) • shaved celery salad (*see p92*) • marinated olives with orange (*see p30*)

PARTNER WITH

Mushroom and chestnut soup (*see p38*) • chunky eggplant sticks (*see p23*) • artichoke puff-pastry bites (*see p196*)

Baby beets and bresaola
with creamy horseradish dressing

The skin of baby beets is delicious when roasted, so don't spend time peeling when making this pretty crimson and green salad.

1 Preheat the oven to 400°F (200°C). Place the beets on a large piece of heavy foil. Add the thyme sprigs, salt and pepper, and spoon on the olive oil. Fold over the foil to create an airtight package. Bake for 45 minutes, or until easily pierced with a knife. Unwrap, trim the stems, and cut each beet in half. Place in a bowl and sprinkle with the red wine vinegar.

2 Mix the dressing ingredients in a small bowl. Divide the arugula, bresaola, and halved beets between 8 small plates. Just before serving, spoon on the dressing, and sprinkle with chives or parsley.

Prepare ahead

The beets can be roasted and the dressing prepared earlier on the same day you plan to serve them—just keep them covered and refrigerated. Arrange just before serving.

INGREDIENTS

10–12 baby beets or
4 medium-sized beets,
cut into quarters

2 thyme sprigs

½ tsp each salt and pepper

3 tbsp extra-virgin olive oil

2 tbsp red wine vinegar

Small handful arugula leaves

4 slices bresaola, prosciutto, or serrano ham, torn in half

Chopped fresh chives or parsley, to garnish

Dressing

1 tbsp grated horseradish, bottled or fresh

5 tbsp crème fraîche or sour cream

1 tsp white wine or rice vinegar

1 tbsp lemon juice

1 tbsp grated lemon zest

½ tsp each salt and pepper

Preparation time 15 minutes
Cooking time 45 minutes
Makes 8 small plates

BUY AND ARRANGE	PARTNER WITH
Tomato and feta skewers (see p31) • marinated anchovies (see p30) • spice-dusted shrimp (see p148)	Yellow lentil soup (see p44) • serrano-wrapped shrimp (see p108) • peach and raspberry chips (see p212)

Broiled baby eggplants
with miso dressing

Miso is a fermented soybean paste from Japan. Its nutty, salty tones complement the subtlety of eggplant. Use baby eggplants if you can—they have a silky, soft texture.

1 Preheat the oven to 400°F (200°C). If using baby eggplants, slice in half lengthwise, leaving stems on. For larger eggplants, cut into 1-in (2½-cm) slices. Cut a crisscross pattern into the flesh. Drizzle with the oil and season with the salt and pepper. Transfer to a nonstick baking sheet and bake for about 20 minutes, until golden.

2 Preheat the broiler to high. In a small bowl, combine the dressing ingredients, mixing well. Spread the mixture thickly onto the eggplants and sprinkle with the sesame seeds. Place under the broiler for 1–2 minutes. Serve garnished with the scallions and accompanied by any leftover dressing as a dip.

Prepare ahead

The dressing can be made the night before you need it, and the eggplants can be roasted 4 hours before grilling and serving.

INGREDIENTS

12 baby, or 4 small eggplants

2 tbsp vegetable or olive oil

½ tsp each salt and pepper

1 tsp sesame seeds

4 scallions, chopped, to garnish

Dressing

⅓ cup miso paste (preferably light-colored)

3 tbsp sugar

3 tbsp sake

Juice of ½ lime and ½ lemon

½ tsp chili pepper flakes, or ½ fresh red chili pepper, finely chopped

Preparation time 10 minutes

Cooking time 22 minutes

Makes 8 servings

BUY AND ARRANGE

Watercress salad with spring onion (see p93) • fresh oysters (see p148) • caramelized grilled pineapple (see p215)

PARTNER WITH

Roasted butternut squash (see p162) • Peking seared duck rolls (see p180) • seared sesame tuna (see p138)

Quick vegetables
buy-and-arrange ideas to create simple recipes

Often it is the simplest dishes that work best, especially if you find high-quality, in-season produce. Vegetable dishes can be a sticking point for many people, so time-saving ideas are the answer—simply roast or broil and season well. Be adventurous and try something new, such as the roasted shallots—so simple yet delicious.

Roasted sweet potato wedges with cumin

Cut 3 large, peeled sweet potatoes into wedges, about 1 in (2.5 cm) in size, and drizzle with 2 tablespoons olive oil and 2 teaspoons whole cumin seeds. Roast in an oven preheated to 400°F (200°C) for 30–40 minutes, until crispy. Shake the baking tray frequently during cooking to prevent sticking. Serve warm.

Piquillo peppers with sherry vinegar

Drain a 7-oz (200-g) jar of Spanish piquillo peppers or roasted red peppers and slice them thinly. Mix the peppers with 1 teaspoon sherry vinegar, 1 tablespoon extra-virgin olive oil, and 1 small handful chopped parsley, then season with salt and pepper. Serve with toasted bread.

Roasted asparagus with soy sauce, balsamic vinegar, and walnut oil

Trim 2 bunches of asparagus and toss them with 1 teaspoon soy sauce, 1 tablespoon walnut oil, and 1 tablespoon balsamic vinegar, then season with salt and pepper. Roast them in the oven for about 15 minutes at 400°F (200°C) until golden. Alternatively, cook in a broiler pan and pour the vinaigrette over afterward. Serve warm.

Grilled chicory with vinegar

Slice 2–3 small heads of chicory in half lengthwise. Brush each half with 1 teaspoon olive oil, then season with salt and pepper. Put the chicory in a broiler pan with the cut side facing downward and broil them until golden. Splash each half with some sherry or balsamic vinegar after cooking. Place them on a serving dish to be picked up and eaten by hand.

Roasted peppers with garlic

Cut 3 red peppers in half and remove the seeds. Fill each half with a few halved cherry tomatoes, 2 slices of a garlic clove, 3 capers, and 2–3 basil leaves, then season with salt and pepper. Bake at 400°F (200°C) for 30–40 minutes, until golden. Tear 2 fresh mozzarella balls into pieces. Top the pepper halves with the mozzarella while they are still warm so that the cheese melts, then serve.

Marinated Italian mushrooms

Toss 1 lb (450 g) small white button mushrooms with 3 tablespoons extra-virgin olive oil, 2 tablespoons balsamic vinegar, 1 teaspoon crushed fennel seeds, a pinch of crushed chili pepper, 1 teaspoon honey, and salt and pepper to taste. Marinate for 30 minutes, then serve.

Steamed edamame with sea salt

Steam 1 lb (450 g) frozen edamame soybeans until heated through and slightly softened but still holding their shape, about 4 minutes. Serve in a dish sprinkled with 1 tablespoon soy sauce and 1 teaspoon flaked sea salt. Edamame can be found in larger grocery stores, specialty food shops, or online (*see p223*).

Carrots in vinaigrette

Peel and cut 4 large carrots into slices, blanch in boiling water until al dente, then place in a dish. In a bowl, mix together 3 tablespoons red wine vinegar, 5 tablespoons extra-virgin olive oil, 1 chopped clove garlic, and 1 small handful chopped parsley. Pour over the carrots and marinate chilled for at least 1 hour or overnight.

Avocado with balsamic vinegar and dill

Cut 3–4 avocados in half, remove the stone, and rub with a little lemon juice. Into each half add 1 teaspoon extra-virgin olive oil, 1 teaspoon balsamic vinegar, and 1 small handful freshly chopped dill, then season with salt and pepper. Serve immediately.

Roasted shallots

In a baking tray, toss 15 small to medium-sized unpeeled shallots with 1 tablespoon olive oil and roast for 30 minutes at 400°F (200°C). Serve warm and allow guests to peel them as they eat.

Roasted new potatoes with smoky paprika

Roasted new potatoes with smoky paprika

In a bowl, toss 1 lb (450 g) small new potatoes with 2 tablespoons olive oil and 1 teaspoon either smoky paprika, pimenton, or chili powder. Roast them for 30 minutes in an oven preheated to 400°F (200°C). Serve with a dip and toothpicks to pick them up.

Radishes with tapenade and chilled butter

Trim the bottoms off 3–4 handfuls of radishes, but leave the tops untrimmed to be used as handles. Serve them with a good-quality black olive tapenade and some chilled butter to dip.

Each small parcel that you prepare is a present with a succulent treasure waiting inside. First, select your favorite wrapper from the vast selection available, such as tortillas, rice papers, and pastries. Then create a piquant filling of vegetables, seafood, or cheese, and get rolling.

Wrapped, tied, and rolled

Seafood spring rolls
with sweet chili and cilantro sauce

Take a bite of one of these Vietnamese specialties and you'll
be overwhelmed by an intense aroma of fresh herbs. Unlike
fried rolls, these wrappers are made of rice paper.

1   Arrange the seafood, onion, carrots, ginger, and herbs in separate
piles on a tray. Place a large clean dish towel on a work surface,
and fill a medium-sized bowl with hot water.

2   Drop one rice paper wrapper at a time into the hot water for about
30 seconds. When soft and pliable, place the wrapper on the dish
towel and dab off excess water with another towel. Fill the lower
side of the wrapper with 1 tablespoon of seafood, and lay some
onion, carrot, and herbs across the other side, allowing them to
protrude from the top of the wrapper. Fold over the lower part of
the wrapper around the seafood, then fold in the sides and roll up
to make a tight parcel. Repeat with the remaining wrappers. Serve
with sweet chili and cilantro sauce.

Prepare ahead

The rolls may be made the night before. Cover with 2 pieces of
paper towel and wrap in plastic wrap, then store in the refrigerator.

INGREDIENTS

8 oz (250 g) mixed cooked
seafood such as white crab
meat, peeled shrimp, or
lobster meat

1 red onion, thinly sliced

2 large carrots, julienned

2-in (5-cm) piece fresh ginger,
very thinly sliced

20 cilantro sprigs, about
3 in (7½ cm) long

40 fresh mint leaves

20 x 6-in- (15-cm-) wide
circular rice paper wrappers

1 recipe sweet chili and cilantro
sauce (see p218) or bottled
sweet chili dipping sauce,
to serve

Preparation time 1 hour
Makes 20 rolls

BUY AND ARRANGE

Shrimp and cucumber skewers
(see p149) • watercress salad
with spring onion (see p93) •
sliced watermelon (see p215)

PARTNER WITH

Thai corn fritters (see p26) •
lemongrass beef skewers
(see p104) • seared duck and
mango salad (see p90)

Soft shell steak tacos
with smoky tomatillo sauce

Tomatillos look like little green tomatoes covered in sticky paper. If fresh tomatillos are not available, use 11 oz (300 g) canned tomatillos, which are equivalent to 1 lb (450 g) fresh.

1   In a large bowl, mix together the olive oil, chili powder, salt, and pepper. Add the meat, turn to coat, and marinate for 30 minutes.

2   Preheat the broiler and soak the onions in the lime juice. While they soak, pan-fry the garlic for 8 minutes in a dry nonstick frying pan over moderate heat. Stir until soft and blackened. Leave to cool, then peel. Place the tomatillos on a baking sheet and cook under the broiler for 8 minutes, until blackened. Leave to cool.

3   Place the remaining sauce ingredients in a food processor or blender. Puree coarsely. Fold in the onion mixture and set aside.

4   Heat the broiler to medium. Remove the meat from its marinade and broil for 3 minutes on each side, or until medium rare. Cover with foil, leave to rest for 10 minutes, then slice thinly across the grain. Toss the scallions in a little oil, season with salt and pepper, and broil briefly. Fill the taco shells with the steak slices, smoky tomatillo sauce, crème fraîche, carrot escabeche (if using), onions, and lettuce. Serve immediately. Alternatively, allow guests to assemble their own tacos.

Prepare ahead

The steaks can be marinated for up to 2 days in the refrigerator. The sauce can be made the day before and refrigerated.

INGREDIENTS

1 tbsp olive oil

½ tsp smoky chili powder

½ tsp each salt and pepper, plus more as needed

2 x 8-oz (2 x 250-g) sirloin, rump or tenderloin steaks

8 scallions

Olive oil, for grilling

16 taco shells

4 cups crème fraîche or sour cream

1 recipe carrot escabeche (see p216) *(optional)*

16 baby lettuce leaves, to serve

Sauce

1 small red onion, finely diced

Juice of 1 lime

8 large garlic cloves, unpeeled

2 lb (1 kg) tomatillos, husked and rinsed

2 chipotles in adobo

Small bunch fresh cilantro

½ tsp each salt and pepper

Preparation time 15 minutes, plus 30 minutes marinating
Cooking time 30 minutes
Makes 16 small tacos

BUY AND ARRANGE	PARTNER WITH
Palm heart and avocado salad (*see p92*) • fruit salsa (*see p70*) • padron peppers (*see p30*)	Serrano-wrapped shrimp (*see p108*) • crab and Gruyère nachos (*see p142*)

Peking seared duck rolls
with plum sauce

This twist on a classic calls for authentic Chinese pancakes, but small tortillas work nicely, too. Be sure to heat them for a few seconds so that they roll without cracking.

1 In a medium-sized bowl, combine the soy sauce, honey, and ginger. Score the skin of the duck in a crisscross pattern and add it to the soy mixture. Sprinkle with black pepper, turn to coat, and leave to marinate for at least 1 hour.

2 Remove the duck from the marinade and dry on paper towels. Heat a nonstick frying pan over medium-high heat and add the duck, skin side down. Reduce the heat and cook very slowly over low heat for about 10 minutes, pouring the duck fat off as it melts to prevent spattering. When the skin is thin and crispy, turn the duck, and cook on the other side for another 5 minutes. Leave to rest for 10 minutes, then slice very thinly into about 10 slices per breast.

3 Spread each pancake with 1 teaspoon of the sauce, then place 1 slice of duck, a few chives, and some scallion and cucumber on top. Roll up the pancake and tie it with an additional chive, or secure it with a chopstick, so that it stays closed.

Prepare ahead
The duck can be left to marinate, covered, in the refrigerator for 2 days, cooked the day before and again refrigerated. The onions can be sliced 2 hours ahead. The rolls can be assembled 2 hours before serving and covered with paper towels, then plastic wrap.

INGREDIENTS

2 tbsp soy sauce

1 tbsp honey

1 tbsp ground ginger

2 boneless duck breasts

Ground black pepper

20 Peking pancakes

1 jar Chinese plum or hoisin sauce

Small handful chives

4 scallions, cut into matchsticks

1 medium cucumber, cut into thin matchsticks

Preparation time 10 minutes, plus 1 hour marinating time

Cooking time 15 minutes

Makes 20 small rolls

BUY AND ARRANGE

Crab and cream cheese dip (see p71) • spice-dusted shrimp (see p148) • caramelized grilled pineapple (see p215)

PARTNER WITH

Thai corn fritters (see p26) • Hainanese chicken (see p127) • roasted butternut squash (see p163)

Saffron feta phyllo triangles
with preserved lemon and onion

Preserved lemons, a Moroccan specialty, add salty
sharpness without the bitterness of fresh lemon rind.
It's easy to cure a jar of them at home, but they can also
be found in specialty shops or bought online (see p223).

1 Heat the oil in a medium-sized sauté pan over medium heat, add
   the onion, and season with salt and pepper. Sauté for about
   8 minutes, until the onion is soft.

2 Add the garlic, preserved lemon, pimenton, and saffron, and cook
   for another 2–3 minutes. Transfer the mixture to a bowl and leave
   to cool. When cold, add the crumbled feta cheese and mix gently.
   Season with salt and pepper.

3 Preheat the oven to 400°F (200°C). Place a baking sheet in the
   oven. Carefully lift 1 sheet of phyllo pastry and cut it in half
   lengthwise, to make a long strip of pastry. Keep the remaining
   pastry covered with a dish towel while you work, to prevent it
   from drying out. Brush the pastry strip with melted butter. Place
   a tablespoon of the filling at one end and fold the pastry over
   from one corner to enclose the filling and form a triangle.
   Continue folding, alternating from side to side, until the filling is
   well-wrapped, then cut the pastry. Brush with more melted butter.
   Repeat with the remaining pastry, and place in the refrigerator
   until you are ready to cook.

4 Carefully transfer the triangles to the preheated baking sheet and
   bake for 15 minutes, until golden brown. Serve warm with Greek
   yogurt or sweet tomato jam.

Prepare ahead

The triangles can be prepared the day before, wrapped in paper
towels, covered with plastic wrap, and refrigerated until ready to cook.

INGREDIENTS

4 tbsp olive oil

1 large onion, finely chopped

Salt and pepper, to taste

3 garlic cloves, finely chopped

½ preserved lemon, skin only,
rinsed well and finely chopped

½ tsp pimenton

½ tsp saffron threads, crushed
and soaked in 1 tbsp hot water

8 oz (200 g) feta cheese,
crumbled

9 oz (270 g) phyllo pastry

Melted butter or oil, for
brushing

Greek yogurt or sweet tomato
jam (see p218), to serve

Preparation time 30 minutes
Cooking time 25 minutes
Makes 20 triangles

BUY AND ARRANGE

Baby lettuce with sherry vinegar
and walnut oil (see p92) •
hummus with smoked paprika
(see p70) • oranges with rose
water (see p214)

PARTNER WITH

Spinach and yogurt dip (see
p66) • yellow lentil soup (see
p44) • cardamom-poached
apricots (see p211)

Pork and shrimp dumplings
with garlic oil

These dumplings are easier to make than you might think, so give them a try. Both gyoza and wonton wrappers can be found at Asian supermarkets, and they freeze well.

1 To make the filling, place the 2 whole garlic cloves, ginger, and cilantro in a food processor, and process well. Add the scallions, water chestnuts, shrimp, pork, corn starch, egg white, and soy sauce, and process again to mix.

2 Hold a wrapper in your hand and spoon in 1 tablespoon of the filling. Fold the wrapper around to enclose the filling, pleating it, but keeping the top open. Press down slightly to flatten the bottom, then place on a plastic tray dusted with corn starch. Repeat with the remaining wrappers, then refrigerate until ready to steam. Keep the unused wrappers covered with a dish towel to prevent them from drying out.

3 Heat the oil in a small saucepan over medium-high heat, add the chopped garlic, and fry for 1 minute, until golden but not too brown. Remove from the heat and set aside.

4 Fill a saucepan with water to a depth of 2 in (5 cm) and bring to a boil. Place some parchment paper in the bottom of a bamboo steamer. Arrange 10 dumplings in the steamer so that they are not touching. Place the steamer basket over the simmering water, cover, and steam for 6–8 minutes. Remove and place on a serving dish. Drizzle with the garlic oil, and serve with the ketchup manis. Repeat with the next batch.

Prepare ahead
The dumplings can be made 4 hours ahead and stored in the refrigerator. The uncooked dumplings may be frozen individually on trays, then placed in freezer bags. Thaw before steaming.

INGREDIENTS

4 garlic cloves, 2 finely chopped

½ in (1 cm) fresh ginger

Small bunch fresh cilantro

2 scallions, finely chopped

7 water chestnuts, finely chopped

½ lb (200 g) raw peeled shrimp

½ lb (200 g) lean minced pork

1 tsp corn starch, plus extra for dusting

1 tsp egg white

1 tsp soy sauce

20 wonton wrappers, cut into circles, or round gyoza wrappers

3 tbsp peanut or pure vegetable oil

Indonesian ketchup manis or soy sauce, to serve

Preparation time 30 minutes
Cooking time 25 minutes
Makes 20 dumplings

BUY AND ARRANGE

Steamed edamame (*see p173*) • Asian cucumber salad (*see p93*) • selection of sushi (*see p31*)

PARTNER WITH

Pork satay (*see p109*) • seared sesame tuna (*see p138*) • passion fruit trifle (*see p206*)

Crispy chorizo quesadillas
with guacamole

Creamy avocado is scrumptious with the melted cheese of these quesadillas. Try making these with different fillings, too, such as grilled mushrooms with goat cheese.

1 Preheat the oven to 275°F (140°C). To make the guacamole, mash the avocado in a bowl, using a potato masher. Stir in the garlic, jalapeño, lime juice, Tabasco, and Worcestershire sauce. Mix well and season to taste with salt and pepper.

2 To make the quesadillas, place 3 tortillas on the work surface and spread with the cheese, chipotle, chorizo or salami, cilantro, and scallions. Top each with another tortilla.

3 Heat a large, nonstick frying pan over medium-low heat and add 1 tablespoon of the oil. Place one of the quesadillas in the pan and cook for 2–3 minutes. When the cheese is beginning to melt, gently turn using a large spatula and cook for another 2–3 minutes. Keep warm in the oven while you repeat the process with the remaining quesadillas. Cut each one into 8 pieces and serve with the guacamole.

Prepare ahead

Covered with plastic wrap, and refrigerated, the guacamole can be made the same day you plan to serve it. The quesadillas can be made 30 minutes before serving and kept warm in an oven preheated to 275°F (140°C).

INGREDIENTS

6 large flour tortillas

12 oz (350 g) Gruyère, cheddar or other hard, melting cheese, grated

2 chipotles in adobo, deseeded and chopped

18 thin slices cooked chorizo or salami

Small handful chopped fresh cilantro

3 scallions, thinly sliced

3 tbsp vegetable oil

Guacamole

Flesh of 3 large, ripe avocados

1 garlic clove, crushed

1 jalapeño pepper, very finely chopped

Juice of 2 limes

1 tsp Tabasco sauce, such as the smoky chipotle flavor

1 tbsp Worcestershire sauce

Salt and pepper

Preparation time 30 minutes
Cooking time 15 minutes
Makes 24 pieces

BUY AND ARRANGE	PARTNER WITH
Palm heart and avocado salad (see p92) • roasted new potatoes with smoky paprika (see p173) • Spanish deli plate (see p30)	Chili pepper gazpacho (see p36) • salmon and pineapple skewers (see p110) • baby clams (see p136) • mini peach and raspberry crisps (see p212)

Bresaola and pear rolls
with arugula and Parmesan

Bresaola is an Italian dry-cured beef fillet produced in a way similar to prosciutto. Real artisan balsamic vinegar — thick, syrupy, and undeniably expensive — is required here.

1 In a medium-sized bowl, toss the pears in the lemon juice, salt, and pepper.

2 Place 1 pear slice and a few sprigs of arugula on 1 slice of bresaola or prosciutto. Top with a little Parmesan, drizzle with balsamic vinegar, and roll it up. The bresaola will adhere to itself. Cut in half for smaller bites, if you wish. Repeat with the remaining rolls and place seam side down on a serving plate.

Prepare ahead

The rolls can be made 4 hours before serving. Cover with baking parchment or wax paper, then wrap in plastic wrap, and store in the refrigerator.

INGREDIENTS

1 ripe but firm pear, cored, halved, and thinly sliced

1 tsp lemon juice

½ tsp each salt and pepper

2 large handfuls arugula

20 small slices bresaola or 10 slices prosciutto, cut in half

⅓ cup shaved Parmesan

2 tbsp high quality balsamic vinegar

Preparation time 20 minutes
Makes 20 rolls

BUY AND ARRANGE

Chicory salad (*see p93*) •
Parmesan crisps (*see p31*) •
fresh crab crostini (*see p148*)

PARTNER WITH

Fried artichokes, Roman style (*see p12*) • spiced goat cheese balls (*see p59*) • farro salad (*see p78*)

Colors

- Charcoal black
- Brilliant white
- Berry red
- Chocolate brown
- Oatmeal tan

Tableware

- Bamboo placemats
- Selection of chopsticks
- Square plates
- Small dipping bowls
- Crackle-glazed china

Japanese style

There is a simplicity and purity to Japanese food that sets it apart from other cuisines. Its genius lies in using fresh, high-quality ingredients rather than relying on complicated preparation. Yes, this is an amazingly healthy way to eat, but that's a bonus—the real story is flavor. The clean taste of this cuisine is accented with miso, sesame seeds, and ginger, but soy sauce is at the heart of it all, lending a characteristic saltiness and depth.

Fresh fish will certainly make an appearance on this menu, since it is a staple of the Japanese diet. This does not automatically mean sushi—marinated, grilled, fried, and roasted fish dishes also play a big part.

Taste is rivaled by the beauty of presentation, too. A Japanese theme means creating a sharp table setting that showcases minimalistic perfection. Think dark, sophisticated colors, such as deep reds and black. Plates and bowls have clean lines and smooth textures. Lay out your chopsticks, square plates, and dipping bowls, and let the food shine. Start the evening by sipping a sophisticated cucumber martini, and finish with a relaxing green tea.

Flavors
- Fresh ginger
- Salty soy sauce
- Refreshing cucumber
- Sesame seeds
- Sweet or salty miso

Nibbles
- Rice-coated peanuts (see p31)
- Unpeeled fresh lychees (see p215)
- Selection of sushi (see p31)
- Shrimp and cucumber skewers (see p149)
- Miso halibut bites (see p140)

Menu

Crispy scallops
with wasabi mayonnaise

Sticky chicken wings
in teriyaki sauce

Roasted baby eggplants
with miso dressing

Roasted butternut squash
with soy balsamic dressing

Seared sesame tuna with sweet soy
and chili pepper dressing

Coconut macaroons
dipped in dark chocolate

BUY AND ARRANGE
Shrimp and cucumber skewers
(see p149)

Unpeeled fresh lychees
(see p215)

Rice-coated peanuts
(see p31)

Crispy scallops
(see p24)

Sticky chicken wings
(see p126)

Grilled baby eggplants
(see p170)

Roasted butternut squash
(see p163)

Seared sesame tuna
(see p138)

Coconut macaroons
(see p210)

Two days before
- Marinate chicken wings
- Make coconut macaroons

The night before
- Make miso dressing for baby eggplants
- Sear, wrap, and refrigerate sesame tuna

In the morning
- Bread scallops and make wasabi mayonnaise and ponzu dipping sauce
- Parcook roast butternut squash and make soy dressing
- Make dressing and chop onion and apple for sesame tuna
- Make shrimp skewers

Cucumber martini

Ideally, you need a cocktail shaker to make this refreshing aperitif. A good quality shaker is a worthwhile investment.

INGREDIENTS

20 slices of cucumber

Large bunch of mint, stems removed

3 tbsp sugar syrup

Ice

3 tbsp dry vermouth

1 cup (9 fl oz) gin

12 cucumber cubes, batons, or ribbons on toothpicks, to garnish

Toothpicks

Makes 4 martinis

Chill four martini glasses in the refrigerator. Place the cucumber, mint, and sugar syrup in a cocktail shaker. Shake, then add a handful of ice, the vermouth, and gin. Shake again, then strain the liquid into the glasses. Garnish with cucumber cubes.

One to two hours before
- Bake chicken wings; keep warm in a low oven under foil
- Roast egplants and coat with miso dressing
- Slice seared sesame tuna; plate with onion and apple, omit dressing
- Plate lychees

At the last minute
- Plate scallops with sauces
- Plate chicken wings
- Add dressing to sesame tuna
- Plate coconut macaroons
- Make cucumber martinis and pour

Half an hour before
- Prepare martini ingredients and cucumber skewer garnish
- Fry scallops; keep warm in a low oven
- Grill eggplants; plate
- Finish cooking squash; plate
- Plate shrimp skewers with a bowl of sweet soy

Pea and shrimp samosas
with mango chutney

Amchoor is dried ground mango and can be found in specialty and Indian food stores or can be bought online (*see p223*). If you can't find it, use lemon juice instead.

1 Peel the potato and cut it into chunks. Place the potato chunks in a saucepan of boiling, salted water and cook for 10 minutes or until soft. Mash roughly.

2 Meanwhile, heat the 2 tablespoons of vegetable oil in a frying pan over medium heat, add the onion, garlic, and ginger, and season with salt and pepper. Sauté for about 8 minutes, until soft. Add the garam masala, cumin seeds, and amchoor. Cook for a few minutes more, then add the potato, peas, and cilantro, mixing well. Remove from the heat and transfer to a small bowl. Stir in the raw shrimp.

3 Take the wrappers and place 2 tablespoons of the filling in each. Brush the edges with egg white and fold over to seal. If using spring roll wrappers, you will need to place the filling at one corner of the wrapper, then brush all the edges with egg white, and fold in from the filled corner.

4 Put the oil in a heavy-bottomed, medium-sized saucepan. Heat until a small piece of bread, dropped in, sizzles immediately. Fry 3–4 samosas for about 4 minutes, until crispy. Repeat with the other samosas. Drain on paper towels. Serve with the mango chutney and garnish with some cilantro sprigs.

Prepare ahead

The samosas can be made and refrigerated the night before. Alternatively, they can be placed in a single layer in an airtight container and frozen for 1 month. Thaw in the refrigerator before frying.

INGREDIENTS

1 large potato, about 8 oz (250 g)

2 tbsp vegetable oil

1 small onion, finely chopped

1 garlic clove, chopped

1 tbsp fresh ginger, grated

Salt and pepper, to taste

1½ tsp each garam masala, cumin seeds, and amchoor

1 cup fresh or frozen peas

Small handful fresh cilantro, chopped, plus sprigs to garnish

8 jumbo shrimp, roughly chopped

20 gyoza or large spring roll wrappers

1 egg white, lightly beaten

2½ cups vegetable or peanut oil, for deep-frying

Bottled mango chutney, to serve

Preparation time 20 minutes
Cooking time 20 minutes
Makes 30 small samosas

BUY AND ARRANGE

Raita with naan bread (*see p71*) • Indian sugar-coated fennel seeds (*see p215*)

PARTNER WITH

Tomato and ginger soup (*see p50*) • tandoori chicken thighs (*see p130*)

Artichoke puff pastry bites
with mascarpone and caramelized garlic

Preheating your baking sheet ensures that the base of the pastry crisps up well. If you are short on time, replace the caramelized garlic with 1 teaspoon of chopped raw garlic.

1 To caramelize the garlic, place the cloves in a small saucepan, cover with water, and boil for 3 minutes. Drain, peel, and slice each clove into 3 pieces.

2 Heat the olive oil in a saucepan over low heat, add the garlic, and color lightly. Drain off the oil, add the vinegar, rosemary, salt, pepper, and sugar, and cook for 3 minutes, until the liquid is reduced to a thick syrup. Pour onto a plate and leave to cool.

3 Preheat the oven to 400°F (200°C) and place a large baking sheet in the oven. In a bowl, combine the mascarpone, Parmesan, prosciutto, lemon, basil, and caramelized garlic.

4 Roll out the pastry to ½ in (1 cm) thick and cut into 20 squares measuring 3 in (8 cm) on each side. Place a large spoonful of the cheese mixture on one side of each square and top with an artichoke half. Fold over the pastry top to enclose. Press the edges together with a fork, dampening the edges first to ensure that the parcels are sealed.

5 Transfer to the hot baking sheet and bake for about 15 minutes, until golden. Serve immediately.

Prepare ahead
The pastries can be made the night before. Cover with parchment or wax paper, wrap in plastic wrap, and store in the refrigerator until ready to cook.

INGREDIENTS

1 small head garlic, unpeeled, cloves separated

3 tbsp olive oil

2 tbsp white wine vinegar

1 tsp finely chopped rosemary

Pinch each of salt, pepper, and sugar

½ cup mascarpone

5 tbsp grated Parmesan

4 slices prosciutto, roughly chopped

Juice of ½ lemon

Small handful basil leaves, chopped

26 oz (750 g) frozen puff pastry, thawed

5 oz (150 g) marinated artichokes, drained and cut into halves

Preparation time 40 minutes
Cooking time 15 minutes
Makes 20 bites

BUY AND ARRANGE

Radishes with tapenade (see p173) • gorgonzola crostini (see p31) • chocolate mint ice cream sandwiches (see p215)

PARTNER WITH

Roasted shrimp and tomatoes (see p145) • three-tomato salad (see p86) • orange and beet soup (see p40)

When choosing which dessert, cake, or cookie to make, please cast aside thoughts of calorie-counting or dieting. Instead, indulge your sweetest cravings. Be extravagant with rich creams, decadent chocolate, sugary frosting, and lustrous, ripe fruit.

Sweets

Chocolate Frangelico pudding
with hazelnuts

Frangelico is an Italian hazelnut liqueur, and it complements this lush dessert very well. Experiment with sweet wines, too, but keep servings small, since this is an intense indulgence.

1 In a large metal or glass bowl, beat the egg yolks and sugar with a whisk until very fluffy. Place the bowl over a saucepan filled with simmering water and whisk over low heat for about 5 minutes, until very thick. Whisk in the vanilla, cocoa, mascarpone, and Frangelico. Continue whisking for 2 more minutes until thick again. Remove from the heat.

2 Pour the mixture into small tea cups or large espresso cups and refrigerate for 4 hours to set. Spoon some whipped cream on each, sprinkle with the chopped nuts, and serve.

Prepare ahead

The puddings can be made the night before and refrigerated.

INGREDIENTS

4 egg yolks

½ cup superfine sugar

½ tsp vanilla extract

4 tbsp high quality cocoa powder

8 oz (250 g) mascarpone

¼ cup Frangelico or sweet wine

¾ cup heavy cream, whipped into soft peaks

½ cup toasted and chopped hazelnuts

Preparation time 30 minutes, plus 4 hours refrigeration time

Serves 8 small cups

BUY AND ARRANGE

Shaved celery salad (*see p92*) • yogurt and dill dip (*see p71*) • spice-dusted shrimp (*see p148*)

PARTNER WITH

Baby beets and bresaola (*see p168*) • roasted shrimp and tomatoes (*see p145*) • mushroom and chestnut soup (*see p38*)

Chocolate cupcakes
with buttercream frosting

These cupcakes deserve a liberal topping of frosting. The decorations, such as rose petals, don't have to be sedate and grown-up—playfulness is the point.

1 To make the cupcakes, preheat the oven to 350°F (180°C). Line a 2-in- (5-cm-) deep muffin pan with the cupcake cases and set aside. In a bowl, combine the flour and baking soda. Put the chocolate in a heatproof bowl and place over a saucepan of simmering water. Stir until melted and smooth. Allow to cool.

2 Using a food processor or hand mixer, cream the butter and both sugars until smooth. Beat in the eggs one at a time, then beat in the melted chocolate. Add the sour cream or crème fraîche, vanilla, and flour mixture, and continue beating until smooth. Spoon the batter into the liners until three-quarters full. Bake for 20 minutes. Leave to cool in the pan, then transfer to a wire rack.

3 Meanwhile, to make the frosting, place the butter in a food processor or mixer. Beat until smooth, then beat in the sugar. Work in the milk, food coloring, and vanilla, adding more milk, if necessary, to achieve a thick but creamy consistency. Spread the cakes liberally with the frosting, top with the rose petals, and serve.

Prepare ahead

The cakes can be made the day before and stored in an airtight container. Spread the cupcakes with frosting shortly before serving.

INGREDIENTS

10 paper cupcake liners

1 cup all-purpose flour

1 tsp baking soda

4 oz (100 g) semisweet baking chocolate, broken into pieces

1 stick (½ cup) unsalted butter, softened

½ cup superfine sugar

½ cup soft light brown sugar

2 large eggs

¼ cup sour cream or crème fraîche

1 tsp vanilla extract

Rose petals, to decorate

Frosting

1 stick (½ cup) unsalted butter, softened

1¼ cups confectioners' sugar

2 tbsp whole milk

Few drops red food coloring

1 tsp vanilla extract

Preparation time 20 minutes
Cooking time 20 minutes
Makes 10 cupcakes

BUY AND ARRANGE	PARTNER WITH
Crushed feta dip (see p70) • watermelon and feta salad (see p93) • tuna tartare on cucumber slices (see p148)	Seared beef carpaccio (see p128) • garbanzo and chili pepper dip (see p68) • citrus swordfish brochettes (see p96)

Chocolate crinkle cookies
with walnuts

These densely rich chocolate cookies are rolled in confectioners' sugar before baking, a trick that gives a snowy finish and a dramatic contrast in color.

1 Place the chocolate and butter in a heatproof bowl over a saucepan of simmering water, and stir with a spatula until melted and smooth. Remove from heat and set aside to cool slightly.

2 In a medium-sized bowl, combine the flour, baking powder, and salt. In a large bowl, beat together the eggs and sugar with an electric mixer or hand-held whisk for about 2 minutes, until pale. Reduce the speed and whisk in the melted chocolate and the vanilla. Add the flour mixture and continue to whisk until combined, then stir in the walnuts. Cover the bowl and refrigerate for at least 1½ hours.

3 Preheat the oven to 325°F (160°C). Line one large or two smaller baking sheets with baking parchment. Place the confectioners' sugar in a bowl. Shape the dough into 1–1½-in (3–4-cm) balls and roll in the sugar. Transfer to a baking sheet and push down slightly with your hand. Bake for 12–15 minutes, until the edges are set but the centers are still soft. Leave to cool on the baking sheet for 5 minutes, then transfer to a wire rack to cook completely.

Prepare ahead
The dough can be prepared 2 days ahead, covered, and refrigerated until ready to bake. Alternatively, the baked cookies may be stored in an airtight container for 5 days.

INGREDIENTS

6 oz (175 g) semisweet chocolate, chopped

¼ cup unsalted butter

1¼ cups all-purpose flour

¾ tsp baking powder

Pinch of salt

2 large eggs, at room temperature

¾ cup sugar

1 tsp vanilla extract

1 cup walnuts, roughly chopped

¼ cup confectioners' sugar

Preparation time 20 minutes, plus 1½ hours refrigeration time
Cooking time 15 minutes
Makes 20–25 cookies

BUY AND ARRANGE

Parmesan crisps (see p31) • gorgonzola crostini (see p31) • crushed feta dip (see p70)

PARTNER WITH

Sicilian artichoke bottoms (see p154) • chunky eggplant sticks (see p23) • baby clams (see p136)

Passion fruit trifle
with strawberries and mascarpone

Trifles are a simple way to showcase colorful, seasonal fruit. Feel free to substitute your favorites, using the same quantities given in this recipe.

1 Beat the mascarpone, egg yolks, vanilla, and sugar in a bowl until smooth. In a separate bowl, whisk the cream until thick but still soft. Fold the mascarpone mixture into the cream and set aside.

2 Cut the passion fruit in half and scoop the pulp into a small bowl. Remove the crust from the brioche, if using. Break up the brioche or cake into smaller pieces.

3 Layer the ingredients into glasses, starting with the brioche, then some passionfruit pulp, strawberries, and a drizzle of Marsala, and finishing with a dollop of the mascarpone cream. Top the trifles with the remaining fruit. Refrigerate until serving

Prepare ahead
The trifles can be assembled the night before, and refrigerated.

BUY AND ARRANGE
Pan-fried chorizo (see p149)
• tomato and feta skewers (see p31) • roasted garlic with warm bread (see p71)

PARTNER WITH
Bagna cauda dip (see p54)
• Ithaca zucchini cakes (see p28) • seared beef carpaccio (see p128)

INGREDIENTS

8 oz (250 g) mascarpone

2 egg yolks

1 tsp vanilla extract

⅛ cup superfine sugar

1 cup heavy cream

8 passion fruits

5 oz (150 g) brioche or plain sponge cake

2 cups strawberries, stems removed and sliced

½ cup Marsala or other liqueur

Preparation time 20 minutes

Makes 8 small servings

Strawberries and figs
dipped in chocolate and hazelnuts

Inexpensive baking chocolate with a low cocoa butterfat content is best here because it doesn't become grainy as it melts. Try using white chocolate as well, or a mixture of both.

1 Break the chocolate into pieces, place in a bowl, and heat over a pan of simmering water for about 5 minutes, until melted. Stir occasionally, until smooth. Alternatively, you can melt it in a glass bowl in the microwave for 2 minutes.

2 Cover a large plate with plastic wrap. Dip the fruit into the melted chocolate, covrering the bottom half. Dip into the chopped nuts. Spread on a plate and keep refrigerated until ready to serve.

Prepare ahead
Covered in parchment paper, then plastic wrap, and refrigerated, these can be prepared several hours before serving.

INGREDIENTS

7 oz (200 g) semisweet baking chocolate

¾ pint (250 g) medium strawberries with hulls left on

2 figs, cut into quarters

1 cup pistachios or toasted hazelnuts, finely chopped

Preparation time 10 minutes
Makes 2 servings

BUY AND ARRANGE

Parmesan crisps (see p31) • hummus with smoked paprika (see p70) • chicory salad (see p93)

PARTNER WITH

Halloumi and sourdough spiedini (see p106) • chunky eggplant sticks (see p23) • bresaola and pear rolls (see p188)

Raspberry meringues
with white chocolate swirls

Follow these golden rules for perfect meringues: Use a clean, grease-free mixing bowl for maximum volume, use room-temperature egg whites, and beat them to a stiff gloss.

1 Preheat the oven to 350°F (180°C). Line a baking sheet with baking parchment. Place the egg whites in a very clean mixing bowl with the salt. Using a balloon whisk or handheld mixer, whisk the whites until they are stiff. Slowly whisk in the sugar, 1 tablespoon at a time. At this point the mixture should be glossy and very stiff. Add the corn starch and vinegar and mix again.

2 Place the white chocolate in a glass bowl over a saucepan of simmering water and stir until completely melted.

3 Spoon the meringue mixture onto the baking sheet to make 8 large meringues. Take about 4 raspberries and a heaped teaspoon of the melted chocolate and swirl through each meringue, taking care not to flatten it. Make sure the chocolate is well incorporated: if too exposed, it may brown during cooking.

4 Bake in the oven for 5 minutes, then reduce the heat to 275°F (140°C) for 45 minutes. Leave to cool to room temperature, then transfer to a wire rack. Top with spoonfuls of whipped cream, the reserved raspberries, and some pistachios.

Prepare ahead

The meringues can be made the night before and stored in an airtight container, layered between sheets of baking parchment or wax paper. Assemble up to half an hour before serving.

Variations

Try other mixtures of flavors, such as dark chocolate with flaked almonds, dried coconut with mango and blueberries, or banana with caramel sauce and whipped cream.

INGREDIENTS

5 organic egg whites

Pinch of salt

1½ cups superfine sugar

2 tsp corn starch

1 tsp vinegar

3 oz (75 g) white chocolate chips or other inexpensive white chocolate, broken into pieces

1¼ cups raspberries

1 cup heavy cream, whipped to soft peaks

2 tbsp chopped pistachios

Preparation time 20 minutes

Cooking time 50 minutes

Makes 8 large or 16 small

BUY AND ARRANGE

Fresh fig, prosciutto, and mozzarella salad (see p92) • Italian deli plate (see p31) • spice-dusted shrimp (see p148)

PARTNER WITH

Cumin lamb skewers (see p112) • orange and beet soup (see p40) • spiced goat cheese balls (see p59)

Coconut macaroons
dipped in dark chocolate

This delicate confection is just right for Mediterranean or Asian menus and is equally good without the chocolate.

1 Preheat the oven to 300°F (150°C). Line a large baking sheet with baking parchment. Whisk the egg whites until they are thick and form soft peaks. Slowly whisk in the sugar, a quarter at a time, and the vanilla. Fold in the coconut, almonds, and flour.

2 Spoon the mixture onto the baking sheet in small mounds of about 1½ tablespoons. Bake for 15 minutes, until golden. Remove from the oven, leave for 5 minutes, then carefully lift with a metal spatula and transfer to a wire cooling rack.

3 Melt the chocolate in a glass bowl over a saucepan of simmering water, or in a microwave, stirring with a spatula until smooth. Using a palette knife, spread some chocolate onto the bottom of each macaroon. Place upside-down on a parchment-lined baking sheet and refrigerate until the chocolate hardens.

Prepare ahead

The macaroons can be made 3 days ahead and stored in an airtight container in a cool place.

INGREDIENTS

Whites of 4 large eggs

2 cups plus 2 tbsp superfine sugar

1 tsp vanilla extract

1¼ cups shredded, sweetened coconut

¾ cup ground almonds

2 tbsp fine cake flour

7 oz (200 g) semisweet or dark baking chocolate, chopped

Preparation time 15 minutes
Cooking time 15 minutes
Makes 30 small cookies

BUY AND ARRANGE

Tuna tartare on cucumber slices (see p148) • spicy peanut dip (see p71)

PARTNER WITH

Crispy scallops (see p24) • roasted butternut squash (see p163) • pork satay (see p109)

Cardamom-poached apricots
with mascarpone and pistachios

Ready-to-eat dried apricots, as opposed to those that need soaking, are smaller, faster to prepare, and a brighter color.

1 Place the water, sugar, lemon juice, and cardamom seeds in a medium saucepan. Bring to a boil over medium heat, reduce the heat, and simmer for 1 minute. Add the apricots. Return to a boil, then adjust the heat and simmer steadily for about 15 minutes, until the apricots have swollen and softened. Remove from the heat, scoop out the apricots with a slotted spoon, and leave to cool.

2 Carefully open up the apricots with a small knife, and fill each with a little mascarpone. Dip each into the chopped pistachios so that the nuts adhere to the mascarpone. Spread the apricots out in a single layer on a tray, and refrigerate for about 1 hour to allow the mascarpone to set. Serve chilled.

Prepare ahead

The apricots can be prepared a day ahead. Store between layers of baking parchment or wax paper in an airtight container.

INGREDIENTS

1¼ cups water

¾ cup superfine sugar

Seeds from 6 crushed cardamom pods

8 oz (200 g) ready-to-eat dried apricots

2 tsp lemon juice

½ cup mascarpone

1 cup unsalted pistachios, finely chopped

Preparation time 15 minutes, plus refrigerating

Cooking time 16 minutes

Makes 20–30 apricots

BUY AND ARRANGE

Radishes with tapenade (see p173) • piquillo peppers with sherry vinegar (see p172) • marinated olives (see p30)

PARTNER WITH

Yellow lentil soup (see p44) • spinach and yogurt dip (see p66) • pan-fried halloumi salad (see p82)

Mini peach and raspberry crisps
with walnuts

Seek out the most fragrant, succulent peaches you can find, or use other combinations—such as strawberries, rhubarb, nectarines, or blueberries—in the same proportions.

1 Preheat the oven to 375°F (190°C). To peel the peaches, cut a cross in each one, place in a bowl, and pour boiling water over the fruit. Leave for 2 minutes, then drain and peel. Cut into 2-in (5-cm) pieces.

2 In a large bowl, combine the peaches and raspberries, the superfine sugar, and ½ cup of the flour, gently turning to coat the fruit. Grease 8 ramekins with some butter and fill with equal quantities of the fruit mixture.

3 In a medium-sized bowl, stir together the remaining flour and the brown sugar, salt, walnuts, and lemon zest. Add the vanilla and melted butter and mix into a soft dough. Using your fingers, crumble the mixture evenly over the fruit. Bake for 35–45 minutes, or until the tops are golden brown and the fruit is cooked through. Serve warm.

Prepare ahead

The crisps may be cooked 8 hours in advance, covered, and kept at room temperature. Before serving, reheat for 10 minutes in an oven preheated to 375°F (190°C).

INGREDIENTS

6 peaches

3 cups raspberries

3 tbsp superfine sugar

1⅔ cups all-purpose flour

1 stick (½ cup) unsalted butter, melted, plus extra for greasing

6 tbsp light brown sugar

½ tsp salt

⅔ cup chopped walnuts

1 tsp finely grated lemon zest

1 tsp vanilla extract

Preparation time 20 minutes

Cooking time 45 minutes

Makes 8 cups

BUY AND ARRANGE

Prosciutto-wrapped melon (*see p31*) • unshelled pistachios (*see p31*) • white bean dip (*see p71*)

PARTNER WITH

Three-tomato salad (*see p86*) • bresaola and pear rolls (*see p188*) • creamy celery and fennel soup (*see p34*)

Quick sweets
buy-and-arrange ideas for fast desserts

Sweets are generally served at the end of the evening, and for that reason alone, it makes good sense to have some simple dessert recipes in your repertoire. When the evening is in full swing, speed and ease are everything. Choose a sweet, or two, to complement the theme of the menu, such as Mediterranean or Middle Eastern.

Middle Eastern pastries

Buy a selection of Middle Eastern pastries and sweets from your local supermarket or an ethnic bakery. Arrange some authentic Turkish delight, baklava, and any other pastries on small plates. If the pastries are large, cut them into bite-sized squares.

Ice cream with sweet sherry and black pepper

Take large scoops of high quality vanilla ice cream and place them in small individual cups or glasses. Pour on 1 tablespoon of a sweet dessert sherry, such as Pedro Ximenez, then grind some fresh black pepper on top. Serve with small spoons.

Brownies with raspberries or chocolate sauce and nuts

Buy some brownies or other chocolate cakes and cut them into 1-in (2.5-cm) squares, dust them with a little cocoa powder from a sieve, and top each one with a raspberry. Alternatively, serve the small brownie squares in small bowls with some store-bought chocolate sauce and a sprinkling of chopped walnuts.

Oranges with rose water and pomegranate seeds

Peel and slice 3 oranges and place them in a shallow serving dish. Sprinkle on a small handful of pomegranate seeds and top with 1 tablespoon rose water. Serve with natural plain yogurt, if desired.

Caramelized grilled pineapple

Cut 1 small pineapple into thick slices and place them in a bowl. Add 3 tablespoons soft brown sugar, 1 ground star anise, and 1 tablespoon butter to the bowl and mix well to be sure the pineapple is well-coated. Place under the broiler and cook the fruit for about 3 minutes on each side until golden. Serve in small dishes with a scoop of high quality vanilla ice cream.

Lemon curd spread on toasted brioche

Buy some lemon curd, chocolate hazelnut spread, and caramel sauce, such as dulce de leche. Slice a brioche loaf into pieces, toast them, then slice again into 2-in (5-cm) squares. Serve them with one, or a selection, of the toppings in bowls for guests to help themselves. Serve warm or at room temperature.

Fruit fools

Process ½ lb (250 g) of a mixture of fruit, such as raspberries, strawberries, blueberries, or mango, in a food processor or blender until pureed. Transfer the fruit to a bowl and gently fold in 4 cups of softly-whipped heavy cream. Serve the mixture in small glasses, topped with whole berries and some small cookies.

Biscotti, mascarpone, and dessert wine

Visit your local deli or supermarket to buy some Italian biscotti or a selection of colorfully wrapped amaretti cookies. Present the cookies on a serving dish with a spoonful of mascarpone and a glass of dessert wine, such as Vin Santo, to dip them in.

Exotic fruit salad

Chocolate mint ice cream sandwiches

Spoon 2 tablespoons of mint ice cream onto a thin chocolate cookie and spread it out. Top with another cookie to create a sandwich. Freeze before serving to make them easier to eat. Experiment by choosing different flavors of ice cream and cookies.

Unpeeled lychees and freshly sliced fruit

Buy a mixture of the freshest fruit you can find, such as unpeeled lychees, kiwi fruit, mango, pineapple, papaya, or watermelon. Slice them thickly, or into bite-sized chunks, and serve them in small bowls.

Exotic fruit salad

Chop up a combination of exotic fruit, such as mango, melon, pineapple, or papaya into 2-in (5-cm) pieces. Aim for about 5 large handfuls of a mixture of fruit and place it in a bowl. Add 2 tablespoons toasted dried coconut and the juice of 1 lime, and toss well to coat. Serve in small bowls.

Indian sugar-coated fennel seeds

Packs of sugar-coated fennel seeds can be found in Indian or Middle Eastern food shops, or they can be bought online (see p223). Serve the seeds in small bowls.

Useful recipes
sauces, salsas, chutneys, and chips

Dill yogurt sauce

14 oz (400 g) plain, natural, full-fat yogurt

2 tbsp fresh dill

½ tsp each salt and pepper

Beat the yogurt until smooth, then stir in the dill, salt, and pepper.

Carrots escabeche with jalapeños

1¼ cups cider vinegar

⅓ cup water

2 tbsp vegetable oil

1 tbsp salt

1 tbsp sugar

1 tsp dried oregano

3 medium carrots, peeled and finely diced

1 jalapeño pepper or other small green chili pepper, thickly sliced

1 small yellow onion, finely diced

2 garlic cloves, halved

In a medium-sized saucepan, heat the vinegar, water, oil, salt, sugar, and oregano, and bring to a boil. Place the remaining ingredients in a large sealable container. Pour in the liquid, allow it to cool, close the lid, then refrigerate (it will keep for up to 2 weeks).

Fresh mint and parsley sauce

2 large handfuls fresh mint leaves, finely chopped

2 tbsp finely chopped flat-leaf parlsey

1 tsp capers, finely chopped

1 anchovy, finely chopped

1 tbsp superfine sugar

3 tbsp red wine vinegar

4 tbsp extra-virgin olive oil

Mix all of the ingredients together in a small bowl, stirring well to combine.

Lime and chili pepper dressing or dipping sauce

3 tbsp palm or brown sugar

½ medium red chili pepper, deseeded and finely chopped

2 garlic cloves, finely chopped

1 tbsp peeled and finely chopped fresh ginger

½ cup lime juice

2 tbsp fish sauce

Crush the sugar, chili pepper, garlic, and ginger with a mortar and pestle until reduced to a paste. Add the lime juice and fish sauce and mix well. Alternatively, put the ingredients in a small jar and shake well to dissolve the sugar.

Mango chutney

½ cup white wine vinegar

½ cup superfine sugar

1 lb (450 g) ripe but firm mango flesh, cut into chunks

½ tsp fennel seeds, crushed

½ tsp curry powder

2 cardamom pods

¼ tsp cumin seeds

¼ tsp nigella seeds

½ tsp salt

½ tsp whole black peppercorns

Heat the vinegar and sugar over low heat, stirring with a wooden spoon, until the sugar has dissolved. Add all of the remaining ingredients and stir again. Simmer for about 30 minutes, until thickened. Cool and remove the cardamom pods. Set aside until needed.

Mango mint dipping sauce

1 large mango, peeled and cut into chunks

Juice of 2 limes

1 thumb-sized red chili pepper, deseeded and finely diced

Small handful mint leaves

Small handful fresh cilantro, roughly chopped

1 tsp fish sauce

2 tbsp yogurt

Place all of the ingredients in a food processor and blend until smooth.

Pita crisps

6 white pita breads

4 tbsp olive oil

1½ tsp salt

1 tsp black pepper

Preheat the oven to 350°F (180°C). Use scissors to cut the outer, curved edges off the pitas. Split each one open and then cut out large triangles of bread. Place on a large roasting pan and drizzle with the oil, tossing to coat evenly. Sprinkle with the salt and pepper and bake for 8–10 minutes, until crisp and golden brown. Allow to cool, then store in an airtight container for up to 3 days.

Pomegranate dipping sauce

¼ cup pomegranate molasses

2 cloves garlic, crushed

¼ tsp ground cinnamon

Mango chutney

½ tsp salt

3 tbsp extra-virgin olive oil

1 tsp sugar

Combine all of the ingredients together in a small bowl.

Ponzu dipping sauce

1 cup soy sauce

4 tbsp sugar

Juice of ½ lime

Juice of ½ lemon

1 green onion, chopped

In a medium-sized saucepan, heat the soy sauce and sugar until the sugar dissolves. Add the lime and lemon juice and allow to cool to room temperature, then stir in the chopped onion.

Saffron lemon aioli

½ garlic clove

½ tsp salt

½ tsp crushed saffron threads

1 egg yolk

⅓ cup extra-virgin olive oil

⅓ cup vegetable oil

Juice of ½ lemon

Place the garlic, salt, and saffron threads in a mortar and pestle or food processor. Crush or process to a paste, then add the egg. Slowly add the two oils with the motor running, or as you stir, then the lemon juice. The mixture should be thick and emulsified. Cover with plastic wrap and refrigerate until needed.

Sticky cucumber and peanut dipping sauce

⅔ cup rice vinegar

½ cup sugar

½ tsp salt

1 small cucumber, deseeded and finely diced

2 shallots, finely sliced

1 thumb-sized red chili pepper, finely chopped

1 garlic clove, chopped

3 tbsp roasted peanuts, finely crushed

2 tsp chopped fresh cilantro

Place the vinegar, sugar, and salt in a medium saucepan and heat, stirring until the sugar has completely dissolved. Boil for around 6–7 minutes, or until a thin syrup has formed. When the syrup has cooled, add the cucumber, shallots, chili pepper, garlic, peanuts, and cilantro, and mix together thoroughly.

Sweet chili pepper and cilantro sauce

1 cup rice vinegar

¾ cup superfine sugar

1 tsp salt

3 garlic cloves, finely chopped

3 thumb-sized red chili peppers, deseeded and finely chopped

3 tbsp finely chopped fresh cilantro

In a medium-sized saucepan, heat the vinegar and sugar and bring to a boil. Simmer for about 3 minutes, until a syrup forms. Pour into a bowl and leave to cool. Add the remaining ingredients and mix well.

Spicy peanut sauce

1 tsp vegetable oil

1 clove garlic, chopped

1 tsp crushed red chili pepper or chili bean paste

¼ cup hoisin sauce

2 tbsp smooth peanut butter

1 tsp tomato paste

1 tsp sugar

⅓ cup coconut milk, plus extra as necessary

Heat the oil in a medium-sized saucepan until hot. Add the garlic and pepper and stir for just 5 seconds. Add all of the

remaining ingredients and continue stirring until smooth. Add more coconut milk if the mixture is too thick.

Sweet soy and chili pepper dipping sauce

3 tbsp ketchup manis, or use 3 tbsp soy sauce mixed with 1 tbsp brown sugar

1 thumb-sized red chili pepper, deseeded and stem removed

2 garlic cloves

1 in (2.5 cm) fresh ginger, peeled and roughly chopped

Juice of 2 limes

2 tbsp superfine sugar

Place all of the ingredients in a food processor and puree until fairly smooth. The mixture may also be chopped by hand.

Sweet tomato jam

2 tbsp olive oil

2 cloves garlic, finely chopped

2 tbsp finely chopped fresh ginger

½ cup cider vinegar

1 cinnamon stick

1½ lb (700 g) peeled tomatoes, chopped or pureed

4 tbsp brown sugar

1 tsp ground cumin

¼ tsp cayenne pepper

Pinch ground cloves

Place the oil in a large saucepan, add the garlic and ginger, and sauté until golden. Add the vinegar and allow the mixture to sizzle for about 1–2 minutes. Pour in the remaining ingredients. Cover with a lid or splatter guard and cook for 30 minutes, until thick. Allow to cool before serving.

Tamarind and ginger dipping sauce

2 tbsp dried tamarind pulp or 5 oz (150 g) bottled puree

½ cup hot water

2 tbsp brown sugar

½ tsp ground cumin

½ tsp ground fennel

½ tsp finely grated fresh ginger

1 tsp lemon juice to taste

½ tsp salt

Place the tamarind pulp in a bowl and cover with the water. Leave to soak until the water cools. Mash the pulp until dissolved thoroughly in the water. Sieve the mixture, pushing all the pulp through and discarding the fiber and seeds. Add a little more water

Wasabi mayonnaise

to increase the amount, if necessary. If using the bottled puree, mix with 3 tablespoons water. Add the remaining ingredients and stir well.

Wasabi mayonnaise

2 tbsp prepared wasabi paste

1 large egg, at room temperature

1 tbsp rice vinegar

1½ tbsp soy sauce

½ tsp ground white pepper

1 cup groundnut oil

Place all of the ingredients except the oil in a food processor and blend together

quickly. Slowly drizzle in the oil through the feed tube until the mixture is emulsified. Transfer the mayonnaise to a bowl, cover, and refrigerate. If you're short on time, simply add the wasabi paste, rice vinegar, and soy sauce to 1 cup of a high quality mayonnaise and mix well.

Index

Page numbers in *italics* refer to illustrations and their captions

Useful Addresses

CHEESES

www.cheesesupply.com

A full selection of cheese accessories and cheeses from around the world (a great place to order halloumi). *See also Oils and Vinegars.*

EXTENSIVE RANGE

www.ethnicgrocer.com

This website is a virtual one-stop food shop for almost any unusual ingredient. Shop here for products by well-known manufacturers, including miso paste, ketchup manis, preserved lemons, sherry vinegar, pomegranate molasses, tamarind, and pimento parika.

www.wildlydelicious.com

This Canadian company sells an array of products including oils, vinegars, tapenades, mustards, sauces and marinades, spice rubs, sea salts, and savory seasonings.

www.sasselections.com

SAS Selections is a Canadian distributor of a wide range of international gourmet food products—from olive oils to pasta—and from exotic sea salts to sweets.

LATIN

www.chiletoday.com

Wide range of dried Mexican chili peppers, salsas, chipotles in adobo, and dried spices. Website also includes recipes and detailed descriptions of each chili.

MEDITERRANEAN

www.formaggiokitchen.com

Extensive Italian and Mediterranean products including cheeses; farro and other grains; extra-virgin olive oils; vinegars, such as sherry and cabernet sauvignon; and mustards.

www.spanishtable.com

Wonderful selection of Spanish ingredients including padron peppers; saffron; pimenton paprika; sherry or cabernet sauvignon vinegar; piquillo peppers; and extra-virgin olive oils.

MIDDLE EASTERN

www.kalustyans.com

Very good selection of Middle Eastern products including preserved lemons; rose and orange water; pistachios; pomegranate molasses; dried spices; harissa; and olives.

OILS AND VINEGARS

www.zingermans.com

Extensive range of the best artisan-quality vinegars and oils from all over the world. Also carries other useful items such as Poilane sourdough bread from France.

www.dibruno.com

A variety of quality oil and vinegar, plus over 500 gourmet cheeses.

SPICES

www.penzeys.com

Carries an exhaustive list of spices from all over the globe. Excellent quality and freshness.

www.spicesetc.com

A large selection of spices packaged in small and wholesale quantities.

Acknowledgments

Author's acknowledgments

A huge thank-you to the team that created this book. Thanks to Mary-Clare Jerram for commissioning and supporting my idea to make this possible; to Jenny Lane for her tireless work in project managing and editing—you are a true diplomat; and to Sara Robin, Marianne Markham, and Carole Ash for their long hours behind the scenes in design. Andrew Barron, many thanks for the lovely design and for keeping your sense of humor during the photo shoots. Sian Irvine, for taking such lovely pictures. Lucy McKelvie and her assistant Fergal for preparing and styling the food.

A great gratitude goes to my husband, Patrick, and sons, Liam and Riley, for their patience while I worked many weekends and their willingness to test so many new dishes. To Jean Hanson, my sister-in-law, thanks for her flawless editing and friendship. A big thanks to Emma Leech, Marcia Barrington, Victoria Blashford-Snell, and Lorraine Wood for all your hard work and valuable input in helping me test recipes. Rosie and Eric Treuille, at Books for Cooks, thank-you for your help in starting my food career and your continued support. Also, many thanks to Camilla Scheiderman, at Divertimenti, for your endless enthusiasm for my classes and books and to Lindy Wifflen at Ceramica Blue for the kind loans of plates and bowls.

Publisher's acknowledgments

The publisher would like to thank photographer Sian Irvine and her assistants Byll Pullman and Leo Ackah; prop stylist Clare Hunt; and food stylist Lucy McKelvie and her assistants Fergal Connolly and Tanya Sadourin.
Picture credit: Lottie Davies for the author picture on the jacket.

About the author

An American self-taught cook, Jennifer started her cooking career 11 years ago in the café at London's Books for Cooks. She has a passion for teaching home cooks how to use unusual, bold flavors. She is the author of *The Well-Dressed Salad*, and co-author of *Diva Cooking – Unashamedly Glamorous Party Food*. Jennifer writes each month for *New Woman* magazine and also contributes to publications such as *Olive, The Weekend Telegraph,* and BBC's *Good Food*. She has filmed numerous television shows, appeared live on BBC's *Good Food Live,* and presented two series for Taste CFN. Books for Cooks and Divertimenti both play host to Jennifer's popular cookery classes.